A mitch

June 1914.

WELCOME
TO OUR CITY

—

JULIAN STREET

WELCOME TO OUR CITY

By JULIAN STREET

Author of "The Need of Change," "Paris a lá Carte," "Ship Bored," etc.

ILLUSTRATIONS BY

JAMES MONTGOMERY FLAGG

AND

WALLACE MORGAN

NEW YORK

JOHN LANE COMPANY

The Author makes his acknowledgments to the Editors of *Everybody's Magazine* for their permission to reprint "Lobster Palace Society," "No Admittance!" and "Oh, You Babylon!" Also to the Editors of *Collier's Weekly*, for the right to reprint "Welcome to Our City"

PREFACE

Broadway—that over-lighted part of it, of which I write—changes faster than the main street of a mining town. Its festivities, scandals, shootings, shows, celebrities, and above all its favourite resorts, flicker across the surface of the year like moving pictures on a wide-spread sheet. What was written of it last year, last week, or yesterday, cannot be correct to-day, in detail. I therefore attempt nothing more, in the following pages, than a picture of the Spirit of Broadway.

The second paper in this book—Lobster Palace Society—was written some three years ago, and has to-day a sort of archæological value. Remark the changes that have come, since then! Martin's, at Madison Square, is gone forever; a skyscraper now stands upon its site. The Café de l'Opera has become Louis Martin's, and evening dress is not demanded there, upon the ground floor, but only upstairs in the cabaret and ballroom. What was, in those ancient times, a year or two ago, the Café Madrid, has passed away, and in its place there stands a quick lunch room. The new Rector's, a hotel, though much more pretentious, has not altogether preserved its old time characteristics or clientele. The Beaux Arts, which was a cabaret before the cabaret was discovered on Broadway, has witnessed the rise of other "bohemian" establishments. And so the picture moves.

Even the first and last papers herein offered, though but recently written, are no longer strictly current, and by the time it has been printed, I fear my preface will have become obsolete.

My last paper—Oh You Babylon!—presaged the dancing craze, now raging through the town, and menacing the cabaret. Starting at the Café des Beaux Arts and rapidly passing on to George Rector's, Murray's and Bustanoby's, the mania for restaurant dancing has spread until, to-day, you may see people rise from supper in some of the hotels, to trip the light, and exceedingly fantastic, rag-time toe.

From Louis Martin's—where there is now a ballroom, in addition to the cabaret, Maurice has moved up town, to Reisenweber's, which is, at this moment, perhaps, our principal temple of Terpischore. Three floors, at Reisenweber's, are given over to the one-step, the tango, the turkey-trot and their variants. People even go there to dance at tea-time, in the afternoon.

The dancing craze is not without its striking features. Though they spring from the vulgar sources which I trace in one of the following papers, and are banned in many of the public dance halls frequented by working girls and their young men, these modern dances are not, necessarily, indecent.   The point is that they may, or may not be so, at the volition of the dancers. Certainly their essence is a very close proximity—two persons moving, with the music, as one—much more as one than in the old time waltz or two-step.   The débutante of five years since would have indignantly refused to dance with the young man who held her as he must needs hold her in the dance of to-day.

That is, however, but one phase of the matter.

People of position have taken to frequenting the restaurants where dancing is the attraction—restaurants which are, in effect, merely public dance halls of a more expensive kind than those run for the working classes.   Practically any well-dressed person who is reasonably sober and will purchase supper and champagne for two, may enter.   This creates a social mixture such as was never before dreamed of in this country—a hodge-podge of people in which re-

spectable young married and unmarried
women, and even débutantes, dance, not
only under the same roof, but in the same
room with women of the town.

Liberté—Egalité—Fraternité!

J. S.

New York,
    April, 1913.

CONTENTS

ILLUSTRATIONS

ILLUSTRATIONS

WELCOME
TO OUR CITY

WELCOME TO OUR CITY

I

WELCOME TO OUR CITY

NEW YORK next stop!"

The Afro-American gentleman in the Pullman uniform falls upon you with his whisk and brushes from your clothes—some money. It is his humble way of saying: "Welcome to our city"; of helping you to get acclimatised, so that when our parasitic population pounces on you with all sorts of services you don't desire, you'll follow the metropolitan custom and reach for your change pocket instead of your gun pocket.

Presently your train stops with a long, whimpering sigh, which seems to say: "I wouldn't dump a lot of trusting strangers in New York like this, but I need the money." That is the New York point of view; try to get accustomed to it. We all know that "it's a shame to take the money," and taking it, protest half-apologetically that "we need it in our business."

You and Dulcine alight. You pass your two small hand bags to the station porter. You carried them to the train, yourself, when you left home, but this isn't home, this isn't anybody's home; it's just New York. And in New York one hands one's bags to porters, just to show—well, just to Show.

Taxi? Certainly! Close as the hotel is, you mustn't let people think that *you* are close, too. It would never do to arrive at the hotel on foot. They'd think that you were trying to save money. Save money, indeed! You, a free-born American! Like to see anybody try to compromise *you* like that!

So the station porter takes your little bags

It Is His Humble Way of
Saying: "Welcome to
Our City"

to the taxi and gets *his,* and the taxi driver drives you and your little bags to the hotel and gets *his,* and the carriage starter (in a uniform copied from that worn by King George at the Durbar) helps you and your little bags out and gets *his,* and the bellboy sweeps down like a wolf on the fold, carries your bags in, waits while you register and give your trunk checks to the porter, shows you to your room, unlocks the door, and sets the bags upon the table. You feel in your pocket for a dime, but the bellboy suspects you. He is afraid that it will be a dime. Therefore, before the coin is passed, he leaps to the windows and regulates the shades. If they are down he lets them up; if up he pulls them down. Then he regards them, critically, to see that they balance. All this extra attention has placed you under added "obligations" to the bellboy. The dime won't do. Make it a quarter.

"Thank-you-sir. Anything else, sir?"

"Yes; some drinking water and change

for this fiver—bring plenty of small silver."

"Yes, sir."

He departs. You and Dulcine unpack
the little bags that have been carried by so
many hands. Presently there comes a rap
at the door.

"Come in!"

It proves to be a boy with the change—
another boy. He holds the silver salver pa-
tiently while you collect the smaller coins—
all but a couple of them which you leave
upon his tray. With five whole dollars of
one's money in plain view one must be lib-
eral.

"Thank-you-sir."

"Where's that drinking water that I ordered?"

"It'll be right up, sir."

"Have my trunks come?"

"I'll find out and let you know, sir."

"Oh, no," you say, hurriedly correcting
the slip. "You needn't let me know. Just

tell the porter to hurry them up when they
come."

"Yes, sir."

He exits. At once there comes another
rap.

"Come!"

It is a boy with the ice water—still another boy. He empties it into the pitcher
on your table.

"Anything else, sir?"

"Yes. I want these clothes pressed before dinner." You indicate your dress suit
lying on the bed.

"Yes, sir. I'll send the valet," replies
the boy, eagerly regarding your right
hand.

The hand doles out a dime. The boy
departs.

The porter now arrives, wheeling your
two trunks upon his little truck.

Grunting, horribly, he places them against
the wall and undoes the snaps and straps.
Had you not been in your room when he ar-

rived, he would have dumped them, locks to the wall, and gone away.

"There, sor!" he puffs, wiping from his brow the beads of perspiration which hotel porters can summon as emotional actresses summon tears. You can't exchange a dime for so much moisture. . . .

"Thank ye, sor." He pockets the quarter and exits just in time to let the valet in.

"Have these clothes pressed before dinner," you order.

"And my dress, too," puts in Dulcine, who has opened her trunk and taken out a wrinkled evening gown.

The man takes up your suit.

"I'll send the maid for the lady's dress," says he, departing.

The maid arrives.

"What time do you want the dress, ma'am?" she asks.

"About five," replies Dulcine. "If I'm not here just leave it on the bed."

"Yes, ma'am," says the maid, restraining

This Extra Attention Has
Placed You Under Added
"Obligations" to the Bellboy

her desire to laugh. "Leave it on the bed, indeed! Does the lady think that we maids don't 'need the money'?"

"What show shall we go to?" you ask the companion of your trips and tips, who has been peeping over your shoulder to see how much you hand each menial.

"Let's look over the list in the newspaper," Dulcine suggests. Then, as you move toward the telephone: "Oh, don't send for the paper, dear. That would only mean another tip. Go down and get it yourself."

"Well, suppose it *does* mean another tip," you reply, with some irritation. "Didn't we come to New York to have a good time? You don't want me to be stingy, do you?"

"Do as you please, dear," she replies, in sadly saccharine tones, as she gazes from the window with unseeing eyes.

You give a grunt and hasten from the room. It is so much easier to run away from women than to apologise; and they're so forgiving, anyhow, when you come back. As you descend in the elevator you reflect that there really might be something in all this talk of woman suffrage but for the fact that the dear creatures are so infernally emotional.

By purchasing your paper at the hotel news stand you save a matter of eight cents. You might have saved another cent by stepping just outside the door and buying of a newsboy.

You see, the companies that operate the news stands pay big rentals for the privilege, so, of course, they "need the money." It is obviously quite different with the newsboys in the streets!

Taking your two-cent one-cent-paper, you return to your Dulcine.

"Well, dear; here's the paper. Now what would you like to see?"

After scanning the list, Dulcine remarks that she has heard a lot about the revival of "Hamlet."

There! Isn't it just like a woman to hit

on something serious when you've brought her to New York for a good time? Isn't life serious enough without seeing serious plays?

"Well," you say in a resigned tone, "of course if you want to see this Shakespeare stuff, why, I suppose that goes." Then you heave a heavy sigh.

"Oh, no, dear!" puts in Dulcine, quickly. "I don't want to see it unless *you* do."

"We can find something that will suit us both," you say.

"Of course there's the grand opera—" says Dulcine.

Now listen to that! Can you beat a woman? No, you can't—much as you'd like to! However, you can groan, and you do.

"Pick out something *you'd* like, dear," she says, handing you the paper. "I'm sure I'll like anything you select."

You accept the apology and glance over the list.

"How would you like to see 'The Giddy Widow'?" you suggest. "The ad says 'tuneful music, clever comedians, 100 beauty chorus—100.' That ought to be good, I should think?"

Dulcine assents so sweetly that you forgive her all. Is it not the part of man to be magnanimous?

"All right, dear," you say cheerfully, bestowing an approving pat upon her shoulder blade. "If it suits you, I'm sure it will suit me. I'll run out and get the tickets."

You do run out. You go to the box office of the theatre. Inside the little window is a man with the facial expression of a bored cotillion leader—a social favourite who has stepped in, from his afternoon stroll on Fifth Avenue, to help out a friend for a minute or two.

"Two good ones for to-night?" you inquire.

"Orchestra?" he asks. Hang it! If you

were a New Yorker he would never have asked that.

"Certainly!"

"Nineteenth row," he replies in an icy tone, which seems to add: "Under the balcony, behind a post."

"Do you think I could pick up a pair of good ones somewhere?" you plead.

"Couldn't say," says the box-office man, raising his eyebrows slightly, and gazing past you at a girl who is standing in the lobby. "Might try the hotels." He yawns behind his hand and turns away. Clearly, the interview is ended.

In the "good old days" you might have bought your seats of a greedy, greasy pirate just outside the theatre door. Fortunately, however, the speculators spoiled their own game. If they did not actually kill that greatest of all golden-egg-laying geese, the theatre-going New Yorker, they buttonholed him, jostled him, and robbed him, until even the cynical Mr. James Metcalfe, dramatic critic of *Life,* started a crusade against them, which ended in their being driven from the streets—almost. Even to-day they are not altogether gone. As you leave the theatre lobby, after having been informed that the house is "sold out," a small, foreign-born Jew of the lowest type, will still occasionally approach you and try to drag you to the speculator's lair for which he is a "runner." The neighbourhood of Broadway and Forty-second Street is pock-marked with the little shops in which these gentry ply their trade, asking double prices, or more, for good seats. It is an abuse which no other city in the world would tolerate; and abuse made possible by dishonesty and corruption on the one hand and indifference upon the other. Speak a speculator fair and he will sometimes tell you just what theatre manager he is in cahoots with, and just what bonus he must pay that manager for all of his best seats.

The shrewd persons who "accommodate

the public" by operating hotel news stands conduct no such violent campaign of brigandage. They get good theatre seats and sell them to the public at a little increase of 25 per cent., dividing the graft with the theatre managers.

Who minds a little graft of 25 per cent.? No one but a "tight-wad," a "cheap skate," a "dead one." Terrible epithets, those, in our town, designating as they do a man with little money, or, worse still, a saving disposition. But they have their complimentary antitheses in terms of glory, such as "good fellow," "spender," "live one." Ah! but it is fine to be a "live one"! To take your fifty-cent cigar between your teeth, thrust out your jaw, look the world of Broadway and Fifth Avenue square in its fishy eyes, and say: "Damn the expense! Nothin' too good fer me! I got the price, *I* have!"

You return to the hotel and purchase the desired seats from the lovely lady back of the onyx news stand.   She is more gracious than the box-office man, perhaps, but, like him, she has the air of an aristocrat masquerading, momentarily, as a working girl. The fact is that New York is always masquerading.   Our shop girls have a blasé, indifferent manner which they acquire from the wealthy or pseudo-wealthy women whom they serve.   Our young clerks imitate those admirable beings, the sons of millionaires, as reflected by the yellow journals.   Our real millionaires' sons imitate wine agents, and our real millionaires imitate the aristocracy of Europe, while their wives and daughters imitate, in the matter of dress and artificial colour, the upper half of the Parisian half-world.   The rest of us dress in imitation linen, wool, and silk, and lead imitation lives in imitation homes with imitation marble entrance halls.

From the news stand you go down to the hotel barber shop.   The "brush boy" (who rents the privilege from the barber shop proprietor, who rents the privilege from the hotel management) takes your hat and coat. The barbers who are not already occupied with customers leap to their chairs and regard you with eager and appraising eyes. You select the one who looks least like a Malay pirate.

"Hair-cut?" he asks as you get into his chair.

"Shave."

He looks at you as though deciding to give you a throat-cut, tips you back and lathers you.

"Manicure?" he presently inquires, having noticed that you rolled your eyes when the blond manicure undulated past the chair. You wouldn't mind being manicured if Dulcine didn't always notice that your nails were shiny.

"No."

The barber now starts wondering if, after all, you really *are* a gentleman. As he plies the razor he begins to tell you all about a "cheap skate" who came in and didn't tip him. There is a subtle flattery in this; an implication that, of course, *you* aren't a "cheap skate." You're a gentleman. Any one can see that with half an eye! Now, as you value your face, be careful. Do not let the barber know that you are pleased to hear that some one had the nerve to leave him tipless. Pretend to be indignant.

"Facial massage?" he suggests as his razor makes the last few touches.

"No."

He slams you into a sitting position.

"Hair tonic?"

"No."

The barber has a dismal conviction that his tip will be ten cents. A ten-cent tip is barely satisfactory. Fifteen is better. A quarter and you become a gentleman. The brush boy helps you into your coat and brushes you while you pay the check. You might give him a nickel if you were a "tight-wad," but a dime is *comme il faut*.

Leaving the barber shop you go into the wash room. Here an Italian or a Greek, whose hands are covered with shoeblacking, has placer-mining rights. As you reach out to turn on the water he pushes you out of the way and does it for you. Having filled the bowl, he tests its temperature with a hand which would defile an ocean. Above the basin is a shelf intended to hold towels. But no towels are there. No, indeed! The boy has the towels securely put away in a private safe-deposit vault, in the corner, where you cannot reach one for yourself.

When you wish to dry your hands he gets one out, unfolds it and lays it in your grasp. As you use it, he sets to brushing you, standing close and watching you, like some beast of prey, prepared to spring the instant that you try to run.

You have just been brushed in the barber shop. You don't want to be brushed again. You hate to be brushed. Never mind.

Give up.   For in New York you are at the mercy of the Greeks, Italians, Russians, Irish, French, and Swiss, and there is no American Consul to appeal to.

You step into a rapid-fire elevator and are shot silently to the upper regions.   Dulcine awaits you.   It is time to dress.   You ring for the valet and the maid, obtain from them your freshly ironed clothing, tip them, and adorn yourself for dinner and the theatre.   Then, together, you descend to the ground floor.

The principal restaurant of the hotel is called the Palm Room—in honour, doubtless, of a certain marvellous dexterity possessed by the head waiter.   As you and Dulcine approach the portals you see a crowd of people struggling for the privilege of getting in and spending money.   The more they struggle the more they are held back by a cordon of head waiters, and the more they are held back the more eager they become to enter and have their golden fleeces painlessly removed.

The quest of the Palm Room is like some quest in Greek mythology. There are all sorts of obstacles to be overcome. First among them are the Hat Snatchers, who maintain their gauntlet just outside the door—swarthy, spidery lads, lurking in the shadows of the rows of overcoats, whence they pounce out to snatch your headgear and your outer garments. Hat Snatching has come, in the last dozen years or so, to be a business by itself. It was started, I believe, when Sherry's was started, since which time it has steadily progressed. Impudent, ignorant Greek or Russian boys are usually employed to do the actual snatching, at wages of $25 to $30 per month, plus uniforms in which there are no pockets. And there is a "captain," at $60 per month, to see that they don't hide their tips in their shoes.

It is reported that, in spite of these precautions, the boys often manage to make off with some of their *padrone's* graft, and I shall not be surprised if the uniforms are ultimately abandoned in favour of utter nakedness, according to the latest Kaffir diamond-mining mode.

Like the men-at-arms who served the robber barons of old, these boys do the actual dirty work of plundering, but don't participate in the ill-gotten gains, save perhaps the "captain," who sometimes gets a little share.

It is the "man higher up"—the *padrone,* Head Hat Snatcher, or Hat Bandersnatch —who rents the right to work the checking graft and takes the profits.   According to the New York *Times,* the annual rentals paid to some of the best known hotels and restaurants are as follows:

Hotel Knickerbocker and Louis Martin's, $9,000 each; Churchill's, $6,000; Rector's, the Café Madrid, and the Café des Beaux Arts, $3,000 each; Plaza Hotel, $2,000.

"HAVE YOU RESERVED A TABLE, SIR?"

Figures given by the New York *World* are considerably larger (it's the nature of the beast) and include a droll computation whereby a man's hat, originally costing $5, costs, in the end, as much as that of his wife, whose headgear, though infinitely more expensive in the first place, is not snatched from her and checked.

Having passed the hat snatchers, you and Dulcine begin to jostle with the silk-stocking bread line at the Palm Room portal.

There is a cord across the doorway to keep the eager rich from getting in too easily. And just inside the cord there is a traffic squad of head waiters, who are trafficking in tables. All the tables bear cards marked "Reserved." This merely means that they're reserved for "live ones."

Elbowing your way to the front you catch the attention of a head waiter and say: "Two."

He regards you and Dulcine with a cold, appraising eye.

"Have you reserved a table, sir?"

Shamefacedly, you admit that you have not.

He looks doubtful, but says that he will see what he can do.

Gentle reader, gentle visitor from out of town, you are now face to face with the Psychological Moment of which you have so often read. Place a bill promptly but inconspicuously in the head waiter's palm and you will get into the Palm Room.

"Thank you, sir," you hear him say in low, respectful tones, as he unhooks the cord. You are a "live one"! The human barrier (if a barrier of waiters may be called human) gives way before you. The orchestra seems to play louder. You enter and are led, in triumph, to a table gleaming with silver, china, glass, and snowy napery. The strategic position of the table depends upon the denomination of the bill which you have given the head waiter.   No, he hasn't looked at it yet; he can tell by the feeling of it as it touches his highly sensitised palm.

The musicians, in their red coats, are swaying passionately with their instruments, playing something which sounds like incidental music to the works of Elinor Glyn. Jewelled and scented women—who, though they may spend all their money upon clothes, may not be said to spend it all upon their backs—trail in languishingly, undulatingly, with their gold cigarette cases, and gold mesh bags, and gold mesh escorts. The atmosphere is of jewels, white shoulders, champagne, thousand-dollar bills, and monosyllables. Ah, this is life!

As the head waiter places a menu in your hand, you notice with sudden horror that your cuff is cracked in the usual place. He notices it, too.

"Cocktails, sir?"

"Have a cocktail, dear?" you ask Dulcine.

"Why, Henry! You know I never—"

"One Bronx," you order, hurriedly.

"Yes, sir. Caviar?"

"Yes."

He shows you two kinds of caviar upon the menu. You think of your cracked cuff and order the expensive kind.

"Oysters?"

"Let's not have a great big dinner," says Dulcine.

"But surely you want oysters, dear?"

"No," she answers. "I just want—"

"Well," you say to the head waiter, "bring oysters for two, anyway." And to Dulcine: "You'll want them after you see them."

The dear creature subsides meekly enough, only listening, with a horrified expression on her face, while you run down through the courses and wind up with a bottle of champagne. She had feared that you would do it; she remembers that you did it in Washington when you were there on your wedding trip, nine years ago. You're *always* ordering champagne!

"You know I don't like champagne," she reproaches, when the man has gone.

"Yes," you reply. "I know. But it's expected of you here."

Dulcine sighs and looks down at her plate.

"What's the matter, dear?"

"Oh, nothing."

"Well," you declare with some asperity, "I'm sure *I* can't imagine what it is. I'm doing everything *I* can do to make you happy!"

"Oh, I *am,* dear," she reassures you. Then after the briefest pause: "How much did you give the head waiter?"

Yet you thought she hadn't noticed the transaction!

"Oh, what does it matter?" you exclaim. "Do forget money for a few minutes! Didn't we come to New York to enjoy life?"

She says she'll try. But through the remainder of your meal she only picks at things, as though she thought the hotel wouldn't charge for what she left upon her plate. In New York a small appetite looks so cheap. Cheap! Ugh! How one shudders at the word!

Disgruntled, despite your elaborate repast, you call for the check. The waiter brings it on a silver salver. Observing that Dulcine's eyes are straining across the table at the total, you cover the figures, hurriedly, with a twenty-dollar bill. It is remarkable to think how much there is in our town that a twenty-dollar bill won't cover. When the change comes, you snatch it, without counting—all but the dollar which you leave for the waiter, intentionally, and the two quarters which you leave, unintentionally, because they are concealed beneath the little cardboard slip torn from the bottom of the check, for this purpose.

The waiter takes your tip (plus fifty cents) in the spirit in which it is offered.

That is to say, there is complete ill will on your side and on his. You give him the dollar because you are one of custom's cowards; he takes it as though it belonged to him; as though he was collecting an old debt, and goes away grumpily, without a word of thanks.

Rising, you move with your wife and your cracked cuff to the door of the Palm Room. No one tries to keep you from getting out. The head waiter bows. The hat snatchers leap forward, wait nervously while you search your pockets for the checks, and finally bundle you into your wraps, take their toll, and, having gotten it, drop you so abruptly that you almost feel hurt.

You move toward a revolving door. There is something in its revolutions which recalls a wringer—something to squeeze the last cent out of the clothing which passes through it. Out you go, and taking Dulcine by the arm, propel her toward a taxicab.

"Couldn't we walk to the theatre?" she asks. "I haven't had a bit of exercise to-day."

"Sh-h, dear!" you admonish, thrusting her into a roaring, rickety machine. "Don't mention exercise here. It's vulgar."

"Where to, sir?" demands the carriage starter, clinging grimly to the open door.

"Brainfag Theatre," you reply, with a dime.

He slams the door. With a buck which nearly knocks your hat off, the ride begins. A taxi ride, in New York, is sure to be interesting. It gives one thoughts which must be similar to those of a man en route over Niagara Falls in a barrel—thoughts on the instability of human devices, the brevity of human life, and the benefits of accident insurance. Your taxi twists in and out amid the traffic, shoots up behind other vehicles, hesitates, as though in doubt whether to go over, under, or through, and finally jerks to a sliding stop within a foot of them. In a moment it is off again, charging down upon wild-eyed pedestrians, winding perilously among a maze of elevated railroad pillars, swinging violently around corners, in accordance with the traffic regulations, and finally bringing up in a line of vehicles, moving by jerks toward the glittering entrance of the Brainfag Theatre.

Another carriage starter throws open the door of your machine and thrusts into your hand, as you hasten to alight, a pasteboard carriage check, punched with holes. Lose it; your taxi driver won't come back. Holding up the line, amid the imprecations of policemen and chauffeurs, you pay the man and tip him. And whatever you pay him, you may be sure it is too much. Perhaps his taximeter is overindustrious, but whether that be true or not the New York taxicab rates are too high and everybody knows it. One reason for this is the set of antiquated laws governing hired vehicles; another reason is that (according to a report made by Raymond B. Fosdick, former Commissioner of Accounts) "certain cab companies make a practice of paying fees to various restaurants, hotels, and clubs for the privilege of using the premises adjacent thereto as special hack stands." In other words, the cab companies practically rent from the hotel or restaurant management, portions of the city streets, which do not belong to that management, but to the city. This graft, Mr. Fosdick reports, runs into a sum amounting to more than $360,-000 per year. The Waldorf receives $30,000 annually for cab privileges; the Knickerbocker, $20,000; the Hotel Astor, $10,000; the Imperial, Churchill's, and Sherry's, $6,000 each, and so on down the list. It is another of the beneficent hotel and restaurant man's devices for "accommodating the public."

The lobby of the Brainfag Theatre contains a quantity of large, hand-painted ladies, their heads swathed in gold-embroidered surgical bandages, their bodies in loose cloaks of fur-trimmed Pullman palace car upholstery. Scents marvellously variegated, and escorts monotonously alike, hover about them. All the escorts wear silk hats and fur-lined overcoats, inconvenience being the prevailing mode in the costumes of both men and women. The women's skirts are so tight that they can barely walk in them, the men's fur coats bulky, and their silk hats easily marred and broken. A silk hat in a theatre has about as much chance as a child in a dark tenement. Yet it is in these places that one finds them. The poor keep on having more children and the rich more silk hats. To show a cool disregard for the welfare of your silk hat—that is to be fashionable. Your very attitude seems to say: "Pouf! What does it matter? My man, Meadows, can jolly well iron it out; or if he can't, he can jolly well go to the hatter's and get me a new one. Eh, what?"

A blare of light and music greets you as you pass into the theatre. The coat-room boy, who isn't allowed to come out and openly attack you, leans on his stomach far out of his kennel, and cries imperiously: "Have your coat and hat checked!" His manner seems to indicate that he has the law behind him.

"The Giddy Widow" is a musical comedy, which deals with the comic gaucheries of Hoggenspiel, a German dialect comedian. (Isn't that name a perfect scream?) Hoggenspiel (I haff to laff every time I say it!) comes from Kalamazoo. Kalamazoo is always good for a laugh on Broadway. He is in the pickle business. The pickle business is also very comic. Sometimes I think that it gets funnier each year. An uncle of Hoggenspiel's, who is in the sausage business (also a perfect scream!) leaves him three million dollars (this is the plot, so take notice!) provided the nephew finds and marries a mysterious ballet dancer, known as the

THE COATROOM BOY LEANS
OUT OF HIS KENNEL AND
CRIES, IMPERIOUSLY:
"HAVE YOUR COAT AND
HAT CHECKED"

Giddy Widow. But (proviso No. 2) they *must* live in Kalamazoo. (Here a comic song: "For I came from Kalamazoo," by Hoggenspiel and sixteen Spanish girls.) Naturally, in the second act they all go to Paris—I forget whether it is Maxim's or the Moulin Rouge—and of course the Giddy Widow wants the three million, but hates Kalamazoo. (Song: "The Wildflower and the Bee.") They argue, and Hoggenspiel chews up carrots and blows them out at her while talking. It's a scream! Then there's a song about champagne, with a dark stage, and chorus girls making Hoggenspiel think he's dreaming. Next, the young French officer comes in and wants to fight a duel with Hoggenspiel (it's over the Giddy Widow, of course) and Hoggenspiel is scared to death. That part is awfully funny. Then Hoggenspiel dresses in a frock coat and flat-brimmed silk hat, and pretends that he's a marquis who is famous as a duellist, and the French officer, hearing that this marquis has killed a lot of men, is afraid to fight.

Well, from there they all go to the yacht. Then the head waiter finds out that the Giddy Widow is really his wife, and discloses the fact that he isn't a waiter at all, but is really a rich Roumanian, in disguise. After that they discover that, according to the Roumanian law, they are divorced. So the husband is free to marry the countess, after all. (I forgot to tell you about her—tall, good-looking girl with black hair and a spangled dress.) Then they have that funny song about "Divorce, divorce, you'll all have one, of course!" after which the masquerading head waiter discovers that the little girl with the blond hair, who has been singing off key, in a piping voice, is really his daughter. So he gives her permission to marry the young American naval officer, and *that* part of it is fixed up. Still the Giddy Widow won't marry Hoggenspiel. At last, though, he persuades her to agree

to it, providing he becomes mayor of Kalamazoo. Then he wires over and spends a
million on votes, and turns the pickle fac-
tory into a public dance hall, so of course
he is elected. (Finale: "We're off, off,
off!") Curtain.

It's a bully show. Don't miss it. The
only man I saw who wasn't laughing his
head off was an Englishman, but English-
men haven't any sense of humour. It takes
the Americans to appreciate a joke. We're
a race of humourists. If you don't believe
it, ask us.

The creatures of the night are wandering
abroad as you leave the theatre. Electric-
lighted advertising signs flash and change
like an aurora borealis in the firmament
above. The streets roar and clang with
traffic; the crowded sidewalks shrill with
scraps of shouted conversation. Dulcine
puts her fingers to her ears and says that she
is tired. You bundle her into a taxi and

drive to a celebrated Broadway restaurant, where you pass once more, like grist, through the mills of the hat snatchers and head waiters: tipping to get in and order more than either of you want; tipping to get out again.

You taxi back to the hotel. Tip. You go up to your room and order ice water. Tip. You unhook Dulcine. Tip? No. That is real work—no tip for that.

Presently you tiptoe over, put out the light and raise the window. From the streets, far below, a million sounds waft up to you, muffled by the distance and united into one great dissonance. It is the orchestra of the city, playing its strange lullaby, which puts the New Yorker to sleep but keeps the stranger awake. Creeping into bed, you lie and listen. You fancy hands, all eager to "accommodate," are thrust out toward you, in the darkness, palms up. Eerie voices seem to shrill above the boom-

GO HOME AGAIN—
WE DON'T CARE

ing of the streets.   Listen!   What is it that
they sing?

> "... *It's a shame to take the money,*
> *But we need it in our business.* ..."

It is the anthem of New York.

*   *   *   *   *   *

You and Dulcine may go home again, or
you may stay here in New York—we don't
care which you do.   But suppose you stay;
what then?   If you have children you will
take them to live in a family hotel where
they can enjoy the privilege of playing with
the elevator boys and the waiters, thus becoming, in due time, "cute kids."

If you haven't children you'll decide to
have a pomeranian and a limousine instead.

If you've made a lot of money, you will
find, in a short time, that you have also
made a lot of friends—very fashionable-
looking people, too.   If the women friends
think your wife has "possibilities," they will

take her in hand and make the most of her, teaching her about bridge, cigarettes, and cocktails; showing her where to get those corsets which reduce hips, and those costumes which reduce both bank account and modesty. It is the present mode to reduce everything but prices.

Dulcine will be a surprise to you. Her cheeks and lips will grow redder, she will have a great deal of new hair, a gold mesh bag for her bridge winnings, and an appalling taste for spending money. She won't be like the old Dulcine at all.

As for you, you should enter one of the many branches of the business of accommodating the public. Whatever you may do, see that you do not really earn your money. People who actually earn it don't accumulate much money in New York. Give up all idea of ever having an identity, of ever being more than one of several million distributing agencies for coin. Submit, uncomplainingly, to impositions and insolence.

Conceal, as best you can, your hatred of the countless people who come bumping into you in the congestion of the city's life; for they try to conceal their hatred from you. Remember that New York is the national parlour for the painless extraction of ideals; get a new set made of gold.   And when you see a newspaper cartoon that shows a little man, hopeless and expressionless, with his hat beaten down over his eyes, have a good laugh, for that little man is you.   Then some day, if you follow these directions, and if you started with youth and a strong stomach, people will speak of you as being a "typical New Yorker."   But by that time you'll be too spineless and too gouty to knock anybody down for saying it.

Having been called "a typical New Yorker," you'll be ready for the doctor. He will come and take your pulse and shake his head; and take your purse and go away. He "needs it in his business" just like everybody else.   Then they'll send for Dulcine, breaking up her bridge game (unless she's out in Reno). Dulcine will ask if you have anything to say, and you will whisper, hoarsely: "Don't forget to tip the under-taker!"

Then pretty soon he'll come, in his black coat, and valet you into yours, and give you your last brushing. After that they'll take you driving (out to a little country place they've purchased for you), and it is very likely that the driver will feel worse than anybody else, and that, foreseeing that he isn't going to get a tip, he'll mutter: "Dead one!"

LOBSTER
PALACE
SOCIETY

II

LOBSTER PALACE SOCIETY

NIGHT had cast her mantle over Broadway; not the mantle of darkness and peace, but the gaudy, spangled opera cloak with which she covers that white and glistening section of New York's anatomy called the Tenderloin.

Theatres, hotels, and restaurants were all alight; hundreds of vari-coloured incandescent advertising signs were whirling, sparkling, pouring forth illumined words concerning stage stars, petticoats, plays, whiskies, corsets, and eating places; street cars were banging over switches; automobile engines whirring, horns honking, people howling conversations at each other; the air was heavy with the exotic odours of exhaust gases from motors; life and pleasure were jostling on the sidewalks. For we were at the very centre of the city's gay night life.

On the steps of the Hotel Astor my friend, the Tenderloin Archæologist, halted me, while he cast a ruminative, fishy eye over the riotous triangle of asphalt which marks the crossing of Broadway and Seventh Avenue.

"The historical name of it," he said, "is Longacre Square. George Washington stopped at the old Long Acre farmhouse which used to stand here. But what does the Tenderloin care for history? It remembers nothing but the last theatrical divorce, ten-thousand-dollar dinner, or New Year's Eve headache. When that newspaper skyscraper was built, they changed the name to Times Square. That's the official name. But the only official things that count in this part of town are traffic policemen and head waiters. So the Tenderloin has rechristened its capital again: now it is "Eating-house Square."

The revolving glass doors of the hotel were spinning like millwheels under the pressure of a steady stream of people, flowing in from the twenty theatres of the neighbourhood. We followed them down the corridor toward the large supper room, whence came mellow light and gay music. About the wide doorway of this room stood a knot of twenty or thirty men and women, all in evening dress and eager to get in—a comic sort of bread-line, held back by a plush rope and a young head waiter, who, St. Peter-like, examined the candidates with a critical eye and looked them up in a tome containing the names of those who had reserved tables in advance. The head waiter's book is the Social Register of the Tenderloin.

Watching the sifting process, we saw a couple elbow their way through the crowd. The man's eye caught that of the head waiter. He raised two fingers.

The head waiter bowed, with: "Ah,

good evening, Mr. Feldman." He did not look up Mr. Feldman in his book, but said to an assistant: "Table twenty-six for Mr. Feldman," and hastily unhooked the rope.

Mr. Feldman passed in. Behind him trailed a lady wearing staccato scents and an alarmingly diminuendo dress. Instinctively you knew she had a little, yipping, woolly dog in a flat somewhere not very far away; also plenty of siphons on the ice, and books which were not by Meredith or Henry James.

Clearly, in Mr. Feldman we had seen a man who really knew the ropes. He was not made of common clay but, to all appearances, of *pâté de foie gras* and truffles. He never had to reserve tables in advance. No matter what a crush there was, he always sailed majestically in and found a place. If the regular tables were occupied, a special one was carried in and laid for him.

The "Mr. Feldman" kind of man distributes largesse with a plump and lavish

"AH, GOOD EVENING, MR. FELDMAN"

hand. He has cocktails named for him, drinks vintage champagnes, sends for the head waiter, calls him "Max" or "Louis," dresses him down, and gives him a twenty-dollar bill. "Mr. Feldman" does not pay spot cash in the Lobster Palaces. He merely tips his waiter with a bill and signs his name across the check. Check-signing is one of the most impressive rites of the Tenderloin. It signifies not only that "Mr. Feldman" runs an account and settles by the month, but that he always has aisle seats, down in front, for the first night of each new "girl show," and can play on credit in the gambling "clubs." So it is natural that, as "Mr. Feldman," with a superbly unconscious air, signs and rises from the table, people gaze at him in awe, and whisper: "Who is that?"

"Mr. Feldman" is sometimes young, but usually he is middle-aged and just a little bald. His complexion is of either a pasty cream colour, or an apoplectic purple, shading off to a lighter tone about the prominently upholstered neck. There are deep wrinkles beside the nose, fleshy pouches beneath the eyes, diamonds on the fingers, and very fancy buttons on the evening waistcoat. The whole is mounted upon creaky legs.

While "Mr. Feldman" lives, he lives very high, and when he comes to die, he does it so quickly that he actually interrupts himself in the midst of ordering another bottle. His colour changes. If he was purple, he turns mauve; if cream-coloured, a lovely shade of pale green. An attentive waiter catches him as he starts to flop over on the wine coolers. He has stopped ordering, so his friends know he must be dead.

Obituaries in the next day's papers refer to him as a "prominent clubman" or a "well-known man-about-town," and, like as not, mention a hitherto (and hereafter) unheard-of wife, who lives in New Rochelle or Flushing. Several friends go out there to

the funeral, but not one single head waiter.
The friends think it would be nice to sing
"For He's a Jolly Good Fellow" with the
service. On the way back to New York
they "roast" the widow for not providing
drinks. Then, with a pleasant sense of duty
done, they return to the Lobster Palaces.
By night the Tenderloin has forgotten
"Mr. Feldman" as completely as it has forgotten the old Long Acre farm. If people
should trouble to investigate the matter further—which no one ever does—they might
find that "Mr. Feldman" left, besides the
trailing lady, the widow, and the waistcoat
buttons, six children and a mortgage.

But hold on! This is disagreeable, and
Lobster Palace life is acknowledged to be
gay. Let us dry our tears, go to the Café
de l'Opéra,* and listen to the *haute monde*
of the Tenderloin eat soup.

The Café de l'Opéra is, as I write, the
newest, the gold-and-bluest restaurant in

* The Café de l'Opera is now known as Louis Martin's.

Babylon, though they are building others faster than type can possibly be set. Broadway pronounces the name of the resort with the accent of Paris, Texas, rather than Paris, France. Though it gets the "caf-fay" part pretty well, it rather goes to pieces on "de loppra." For Broadway eats French better than it speaks it.

A uniformed attendant assists us to alight from our taxicab—or do we own a limousine? As he helps us out, he tells us that the remodelling of the building we are entering cost two million dollars. We are prepared to be impressed. And, indeed, there are impressive things about this restaurant. One of them, which has particularly startled the Tenderloin, is the rule that persons not in evening dress are barred from the ground floor. This rule is strictly enforced—"let the chips fall where they may." It opens interesting fields for speculation. It's easy enough to say when a gentleman is in evening dress, for you have only to look at a

waiter and make sure that the one is habited
like the other. But with women it is different. Some gowns are on the borderland.
One fancies that the head waiters at the
Café de l'Opéra may be confronted, now
and then, with perplexing problems, calling
for close decisions. Is she, or is she not, in
evening dress? Have her wait until the
manager can settle it.

Personally, I should hate to be the manager. Suppose, for instance, stern duty
compels him to decide that a lady who
thinks she is in evening dress, is not because
her gown is not cut low enough. Shouldn't
you hate to be the one to break it to her?

Obviously, the ground floor of the Café de
l'Opéra is *the* place.* Those who aren't in
evening dress, as well as many who are, are
sent upstairs. Some of them seem to feel a
little bit resentful. I heard scathing com-
ments on the downstairs diners, and should
like to print the plaint of one particularly

* O tempora, O mores! And now it is the other way about.

pretty woman whom I overheard, but won't, for fear you would think she was not a perfect lady.

" I would of worn my Tuxedo suit," I heard a crestfallen-looking young man say to his tailor-made young lady, as they were transported to the upper realms, "only I had to lend it to a fellow that was getting married."

It's enough to make any one feel crestfallen to come up against a rope and a head waiter, and be told one can't get in. Getting the rope at a Lobster Palace is much like "getting the hook" on amateur night at a music hall. It makes a person feel unutterably cheap, and "cheap" is a word that gives Lobster Palace Society the horrors. Spend money! That is the cry. Marry it, steal it, raise checks, mark cards, rob tills, or kill your poor old grandmother for the insurance; but get the money and, when you get it, SPEND!

People are sheep; let a movement start

and the whole flock will follow, pellmell. Sheep and the Lobster Palace Set are easily herded. The head waiter at an hotel, the restaurant of which is crowded every night, told a friend of mine that but few people came there when they opened. And how do you suppose he got them to coming? Simply by humming and hawing when some one telephoned for a table reservation; by mumbling vaguely the names of fashionable people, and saying, "I'm not sure you can have a table for to-night, but if you'll call up later, I will see." The minute that person thought he might not be able to get in, he was obsessed with a mad desire to do so. He went up to see about it, and when, at last, he was promised a table, a great elation filled his bosom. Such tactics started people coming, and, once started, the movement soon became an avalanche.

What a horrid, clear vision head waiters must have of human nature! How they must laugh together over the antics of the people whom they serve! How excruciatingly funny they must find it to be tipped by men not nearly so well off financially— or even mentally and morally—as are they themselves!

There are many head waiters in these popular resorts who are comfortably off, and several who are rich. Head waiters' accounts are highly valued by stockbrokers. In speculation they often do very well, for, of all the tips they get, market tips from wealthy patrons are apt to be the best. And the head waiters are not the only ones who prosper.

"I get it all back," said a stockbroker acquaintance of mine, as he gave a quarter to a coat-room boy at the old Rector's. "The man who rents this privilege is a good customer of mine."

So we tip them all—though we should like to kick them. And we go away with the feeling that is expressed by the verse from Lamentations: "Servants have ruled over us: there is none that doth deliver us out of their hand."

You may fancy from my plaintive cries that *we* got the rope at the Café de l'Opéra? Not so! We arrived early, opened our overcoats, showed the white bosoms of our shirts to the head waiter (much as detectives show their badges), engaged a table, and hurried out again.

People from the theatres were pouring into all the neighbouring cafés. Crossing the street, we entered the Hotel Knickerbocker. At the entrance to the Grill Room, downstairs, the bread-line had already formed, outside the rope. It looked much like the other Tenderloin bread-lines: all shimmer, glitter, sparkle.

Ascending, we passed through the Knickerbocker bar, a central meeting-place for the men of Lobster Palace Life, who refer to it affectionately as the "Forty-Second Street Country Club." Over the bar is placed Maxfield Parrish's rich painting,

"Old King Cole"—one of the few examples, in the Tenderloin, of art that may be described as chaste. Many Tenderloin restaurateurs and hotel keepers are "art patrons." Their taste in paintings is extraordinarily uniform—ladies out of uniform being the prevailing subjects. It is, therefore, quite surprising to come on "Old King Cole," where one might reasonably expect to find his harem.

Now that we have had our cocktail, it's time to go back to the Café de l'Opéra again; time to sit down, order supper, and take a look about.

"The first spiritual want of a barbarous man is decoration," said Carlyle, "as indeed we still see among the barbarous classes in civilised countries."

If this be true, the Café de l'Opéra should amply satisfy the spiritual wants of the Tenderloin, for it seems to have reached the ultimate in passionate surroundings for food and drink.   But has it?

Some years ago when I first went to Murray's Restaurant in Forty-second Street, I thought that it had reached the ultimate. How Art does progress! To-day I think that Murray's shows architectural restraint. The façade looks like a refinement of a fine old papier maché *palazzo* in the chaste and classic style of Luna Park. Inside, it is quasi-Pompeian, with plashing fountains, mirrors, pergolas, and landscapes set into the walls so cleverly that a man who once sat there from seven P. M. until two A. M. is reported to have imagined himself travelling abroad. They even have lights under the tables, at Murray's, so that a pink glow comes up through the cloth. Quite thrilling! It makes a good place to show your friends who come from afar and wish to gaze about, for dining there is like dining on a stage set for the second act of a musical comedy. You half expect a chorus of waiters to come dancing in with property lobsters glued to property plates.

If dining at Murray's suggests musical comedy, supping at the Café de l'Opéra suggests a big spectacular effect at the opera —the palace of some very festive Old Testament king, like Nebuchadnezzar, or Og, the King of Bashan. The colour scheme is blue and gold, with black marble columns surmounted by golden capitals representing bulls' heads—or are they calves of gold? There is a black marble stairway that is quite the most magnificently heathen-looking thing in town. At the bottom of it stands a gigantic winged lion, with a man's head, in bas relief. The broad stair-landing, visible from the main dining-room, would be a fine place for a priest to make burnt offerings to barbaric gods, while vestals tripped about, à la Isidora Duncan and Maud Allan.

On the large expanse of wall back of this stair-landing the latest and most startling addition to New York's Lobster Palace Art Collection is displayed, in the form of an immense painting, by Rochegrosse, of the Fall of Babylon. This picture was exhibited in the Paris Salon—an institution which, by the way, could hardly have existed in the past few years, had not Babylon fallen, or Leda had her adventure with the swan, or the Elders seen Susanna, or pretty ladies had the admirable habit of bathing. So many paintings of the fall of Babylon are each year submitted to the jury at the Salon that only those which depict that wicked city as falling with a particularly vicious crash of flesh tints are accepted. Monsieur Rochegrosse certainly succeeded. Seldom, indeed, has such a fall been taken out of Babylon!

To place such a picture in a New York Lobster Palace would be daring if Lobster Palace Society had brains or used them. But why have brains? Aren't sweetbreads just as good? So the élite of Lobsterdom have sweetbreads, and, eating, fail to see the writing on the wall.

Men and women stop on the stair-landing to look over the dining-room.   They blend in with the painting—perhaps because some of them are painted, too.   The evening wraps of the living women make the painted ones of Babylon look chilly.   The effect is grotesque, yet it is ominous; for, as they stand there, Babylon is falling about the very ears of these gay, over-dressed, over-fed Americans.

I don't know what the style of architecture is.   The figure of a man like a design from a piece of ancient pottery, which is the trademark of the Café de l'Opéra, seemed to me to be Assyrian.   But a plump Swiss head waiter, who was probably born in the Savoy or the Ritz and came here to help run this place, assured me it was Persian; and no sane man ever contradicted a head waiter in a Lobster Lair.

There's another dining-room, in the same style, on the second floor, and on the third a Japanese tea-room.   Above are several

A Little Man, Who Appears
to Be On a Diet, Is Providing
for the Wants of Three
Healthy, Hungry Women

floors of banquet-rooms,* private dining-rooms, and bachelor apartments. The bachelor apartments seem to be the only rooms in the entire place which have no flesh tints painted on their walls; but maybe they weren't finished when I saw them.

Though it is getting late, let us, before we go, inspect the festive gathering in the main dining-room. At a table near us sits a woman with a figure like a pouter pigeon. She protects her elaborate dress by pinning her napkin to the highest available portion of it, with a diamond sunburst. At the next table a little man who appears to be on a diet, is providing for the wants of three healthy, hungry women. At still another table the arrangements of the numbers is the reverse: three men are with a dancer from a theatre a few doors down the Great White Way.

We see two unmistakable chorus girls

---

* As we go to press the cabaret and dance hall are running, full blast, on the top floor. See page 137.

with unmistakable "Johnnies," besides several suspects with several "Mr. Feldmans." And we are grateful for the presence of a very lovely lady in a rue de la Paix gown and hat; although (as you'll see from the sketch) we saw only her back. Tables, tables, tables; people, people, people; known and unknown; pretty and plain, the seers and the seen. Festive parties; family parties; parties not of the Tenderloin—merely visiting it as they might visit Chinatown; fashionables and would-be fashionables; Americans and New Yorkers.

It is the custom of the Tenderloin to look with pity and amusement at those who are not of it. People from out of town are jokes. Why, one wonders? Why is it comic never to have been in any given place before? Why is it any droller not to know New York than not to know Omaha, or Lhasa? Yet these "typical New Yorkers" —most of whom were born in Philadelphia, or places even more remote—find it droll.

They love to look about a restaurant and declare that certain people, whom they indicate, must have come from Kankakee or Keokuk. They accuse strangers in town of "rubbering." Of course the strangers "rubber." They stare at New York as a New Yorker stares at Coney Island. For New York is, after all, the Coney Island of the nation.

I know a man who was born in West Eleventh Street. He has a gold cigarette case, and a story, which he tells in restaurants, about a man from out of town, who asked a Broadway waiter what pie à la mode was.

"It is pie with ice cream on it," said the waiter.

Presently the stranger was seen to be in great excitement. He had read up the menu until he came to beef à la mode, and was horrified to think New York could stomach such a combination.

There are Tenderloin wags who have

made local reputation and earned numerous good dinners by spinning funny yarns about the people at other tables. I am acquainted with such a man—a waddling edition of "Who's Who in the Lobster Palaces." And, like the other "Who's Who," he is a fat volume, appropriately bound in red. He considers any one who doesn't know the way to Sherry's, or Martin's, or the Knickerbocker, very, very funny. I sometimes wonder if it ever struck him that he—like all the rest of us—must some day traverse spaces in an undiscovered country, which has no Sherry's, Martin's, Knickerbocker. He will be a stranger. Will he, therefore, find himself amusing?

It is after one o'clock. The crowd at the Café de l'Opéra is dwindling. We call for our check. If we have had a large supper, with champagne, for two, the bill may come to twelve or fourteen dollars, with another

OF COURSE THE STRANGERS
"RUBBER"

dollar for the waiter; if a moderate supper, less than half as much.

As always, a spidery attendant from the cloak-room dashes forward with our coats and hats, levies his toll, and passes us out through a revolving door.

All the outdoor lights, save those of the theatres, continue to burn furiously. The "smart" restaurants are emptying; many people are abroad. Some are going home, while others, with the true spirit of deep-sea Lobster Life, are "going on." In the Tenderloin there are always places to go on to. For instance, there is Rector's.*

Rector's remains open later than most of the other "gilt-edged" Lobster Lairs; it is gayer; high life is higher. You're apt to see Broadway celebrities; musical comedy favourites, actors, actresses, show girls, women of not in the least "doubtful character," and the invariable sprinkling of onlookers.

---

* This refers to the old Rector's, now replaced by the Hotel Rector.

Show girls are starred at Rector's; affluent, opulent, effulgent looking girls who think that they will never leave Broadway. A few of them attain a meteoric notoriety through connection with scandals; a few rise to good positions on the stage; a few acquire fortunes by marriage, or by other means. But, as a rule, the Broadway show girl fades and disappears. The Tenderloin which was kind to her last year harvests another crop of pulchritude. She is forgotten, and the road-shows quickly snatch the remnants of her pitiful good looks.

Poor, funny, pretty, dressed-up, painted girls—members of tinkling yachting parties, automobile parties, and supper parties in the land of make-believe! What wonder that they want to try the game in earnest? Have they not their ideals of luxury, as you and I have ours? Yours may be a cigar a foot long, or a porcelain bathtub six feet long, or a limousine twenty feet long, or a steam yacht three hundred feet long.

Mine may be a flannel shirt. To accomplish our ideals we must make sacrifices. To get your yacht you may throw overboard your honest principles; to get my shirt I may give up my literary self-respect. And rest assured that if she wants to live the Lobster Palace Life, the show girl, too, must make her sacrifice.

Rector's is one of the few large restaurants which has not a French name. To be sure, such names as Murray's, Shanley's, and Burns show in electric lights over the doors of certain eateries, and the large hotels seem to favour New York-sounding names: Astor, Knickerbocker, Hoffman, Waldorf-Astoria, Manhattan, Belmont, Gotham. Some of the hotels have special names for their restaurants, however. Thus, for instance, the Café d'Armenonville, upstairs in the Hotel Knickerbocker, is named for the famous Pavillon d'Armenonville in the Bois de Boulogne. The Café Madrid,* Maxim's, and

* The Café Madrid is gone. What was l'Abbaye is now Bustanoby's.

l'Abbaye also take the titles of famous Parisian restaurants which they do not otherwise particularly resemble. The Claremont, at the head of Riverside Drive, and the Casino in Central Park, are the nearest equivalents we have for the *al fresco* cafés of Paris.

J. B. Martin's at Madison Square (recently torn down) was probably, more nearly like a typical big Paris boulevard café than any other New York restaurant, while Mouquin's more resembles a good Latin Quarter eating place. When Delmonico's moved up to Forty-fourth Street, Martin's, in turn, moved from its first modest home in University Place to the old Delmonico building. Meanwhile, the old Martin's, in other hands, became the Café Lafayette, which remains the most truly French of all Manhattan's eating-places.

Martin's at Madison Square was far from being as modest, French and easy-going, in spirit, as in its earlier home. Obstreperous, Broadway infested it, and taught

it to be brazen with success. It was at
Martin's that the comically brilliant notion
of serving nothing to drink but champagne
after nine o'clock, on New Year's Eve, originated.

To get a table at all on New Year's Eve
was difficult; when you got one you had to
drink what you were told. Notices to this
effect were posted in the café. Does this
strike you as remarkable effrontery? Let
me tell you that it is not more remarkable
than the abject apathy with which Broadway
received it. Martin's was almost always
packed with eager spenders; so are the other
Broadway restaurants which copied the
"champagne only" device as, indeed, they
copy everything from one another.

I know a man who once went to Martin's
three weeks before New Year's to reserve a
table for that night of nights.

"Give me your order now," said a head
waiter, "and I will see what can be done
about it." In other words, he might have

said: "If you agree to spend enough money, you may come."

I passed a New Year's Eve there once. No one seemed to mind drinking "nothing but champagne." They not only drank champagne but spilled it on the tables and the floor. Many new acquaintances were made that night—and forgotten the next day. Every one was kind, indulgent. Now and then some cheerful person stood upon a table and bayed at the moon. But then, you must remember, it is not good form, in Lobster Palace Society, to be anything but drunk on New Year's Eve.

The Café des Beaux Arts is a different sort of place. It occupies the two lower floors of a large studio building, midway between Broadway and Fifth Avenue, in a neighbourhood of clubs rather than cafés. Whether the studios above it affect the flavour of the place, I do not know, but certain it is that the Café des Beaux Arts has an individual air which, for lack of a better term, I shall have to call "Bohemian." ("Smart Bohemians," a circular issued by the café calls its patrons.) The word "Bohemian" has come into bad odour of late years, but I know of no good substitute. The Century Dictionary defines a Bohemian as: "A person, especially an artist or a literary man, who leads a free and often somewhat dissipated life, having little regard to what society he frequents, and despising conventionalities generally."

To these requirements might have been added, I think, a soft hat, a flowing necktie, and dirty finger nails.

But what is "Smart Bohemia"? To judge from the Café des Beaux Arts, it is as well dressed, as well mannered as the very best of Lobster Palace Society. It likes good things to eat, good music, a jolly time. True Bohemia, in the old sense of the word, was something which could not be created.

It just happened. And it was frail: stare at it, call it "Bohemia," write an article about it, and it ceased to be Bohemia and became a shoe clerk's paradise. New York is full of such quasi-Bohemia: chop-suey-Bohemia, spaghetti-Bohemia, watered-wine-Bohemia. But the cheap table d'hôte is not a Lobster Palace and does not come within our scope.

The three dining-rooms of the Café des Beaux Arts are moderate in size; snug rooms, with tables fairly close together. There is a Neapolitan string quartette, an orchestra, and a corps of several vocal soloists, all good. They go from room to room, so that you get variety, with neither too much nor too little music. Meanwhile you eat (and drink if you want to) very well, for in these things "smart Bohemia" fares much better than its lowly prototype. Thursday night is the big night at the Beaux Arts, though an effort is being made by the proprietors to turn every night into a Thursday.

The Neapolitan String Quartette

The place is very gay on these big nights; a real *esprit* develops, and one may hear fine singing from a "volunteer" among the people at the tables. Bonci has sung there, as well as other grand opera stars; and Anna Held, Blanche Ring, David Warfield, George Beban, and others of the stage have been known to do a "stunt," from sheer gladness of heart. The very possibility of such a happening lifts the place into a niche which is unique.

But, even on Thursday nights at the Beaux Arts, there comes a time when gaieties must end. To go on to the other places now is nothing short of prowling. Still, if you simply refuse to go to bed—there is the Café Madrid.

The Madrid used to be Churchill's,* the *château d'homard* of a retired police captain of that name, who had a strong aversion to closing up, or closing down, before the crack

* Not only is the Madrid gone, but Churchill has another place—George Rector another—so it goes, from month to month and year to year!

of dawn. Dawn breaks so beautifully upon
the Tenderloin! When the chairs were piled
upon the tables in the other places, the night
owls used to make for Churchill's, where,
unless they got too rough, they could stay on,
and on, and on.

Churchill sold the place to George Rector,
who is not only the son of his father, but a
graduate, with honours, of such gastronomic
establishments as Marguéry's and the Café
de Paris. To have studied cooking under
the late Monsieur Marguéry is equivalent to
having studied singing under Jean de
Reszke. Mr. Rector not only renamed
Churchill's—calling it the Café Madrid—
but instituted reforms as to equipment,
cuisine, and etiquette. The reforms are in
no wise painful. The Café Madrid may
still be called a lively spot in the early morning hours. You may see there people who
are in Lobster Palace Society but not in the
Four Hundred, and—hist!—you may also
see some people who are in both. It is

extraordinary how the two sets overlap each other at the edges—people from Fifth Avenue are such climbers, anyway.

The Madrid is not large, as compared with some other restaurants around Eating-house Square, but it is an extremely busy little place, and is occupied by a peculiarly Lobsterian society. Two hundred pounds of the symbolic shellfish are consumed there every night. For the rest, you may stay till daylight if you wish, so long as you behave. But do behave, for there are two sturdy gentlemen about who are capable of making it quite clear to any one that "rough house" is not deemed *au fait* at the Madrid, this season. Have all the fun you want, but everybody must act "gen'l'mumly."

In the pious times before Churchill's was invented, those who were intent on sitting up all night usually wound up by tacking over toward Sixth Avenue, where Burns and Jack's continued operations. Jack's got pretty wild at times—by which I mean no disrespect to Burns. About three in the morning some sensitive soul, pickled in wines, liquors, and cigars, might suddenly grow boisterous, or jealous, or peevish. Then some one might throw a saltcellar or champagne glass at some one—an act which is termed "starting something." If someone "started something" 'round at Jack's it always ended quickly, and someone suddenly woke up and found that someone was sitting on the car tracks. Jack's is frankly what it is, and the frank, straightaway, strong-arm method of keeping a disordered sort of order there, is not without its merits. It gives an air of wholesomeness—comparatively, at least—that I should like to see in certain other cafés which I shall not call by name.

Dramatic critics know that to attack a play as being vulgar or indecent has the undesirable effect of booming it. There are a lot of prurient people in the Tenderloin, as well as in the rest of the world. That is why I shall not name these other places.

We happened into them late on the night of Lincoln's Birthday, or, rather, early on the morning following. The sad face of Lincoln gazed from the wine-soaked menu I was given. Around us drunken patriots were celebrating, while not far off a hired singer with an execrable voice and an offensively insinuating manner sang a song so vulgar that even this audience did not applaud it. Later came a burlesque of a patriotic air, telling of:

> Husbands dancing hand in hand,
> Shouting the Battle Cry of Freedom!

And it was Lincoln's Birthday!

The place was littered with confetti. Blear-eyed people leaned upon the tables. Glasses were upset. The noise made us dizzy. Five weak-faced youths sat at a nearby table; when an overdressed young woman of the Tenderloin trailed in, one of them laughed and made an insulting remark. The woman swore and sent her escort to demand apologies. He did so, in a genial manner, and in a moment all were friends. And so they settled it—all of them—by having a friendly drink together.

On with the debauch! We saw a woman, appropriately dressed in scarlet, pick up her skirts and jump over a man who was lying on the floor. We saw a drunken young girl half carried from the room. The scene became a dusty, dirty dream, peopled with caricatures and smelling stale as a plush dress on which a goblet of champagne has been upset.

Approximately twenty thousand people have supper in or near the Tenderloin each night. Next year, when newer Lobster Lairs are built, the number is expected to increase to thirty thousand. Several thousand pounds of lobster, and several thousand quarts of champagne (besides innumerable other things to eat and drink) are served by several thousand waiters, every night. And in the morning there are several thousand empty pocketbooks and several thousand aching heads.

You have doubtless heard **Mr. James J. Hill's** shrewd epigram to the effect that it is not so much the high cost of living which ails the United States, as the cost of high-living.

The cost of eating lobster must increase. The demand grows, but the supply diminishes. Millions of pounds of lobster are caught along our coasts each season, but the government statistics show that, despite the work of various fish commissions, the available supply has shrunk more than fifty per cent. within the past three years. In short, starvation stares the Tenderloin directly in the double chin!

.   .   .   .   .   .

With the coming of the purifying, steel-blue light of dawn, we flee like jungle beasts that feed at night.

"Morning Telegraph, sir?"

We take the paper. The boy demands ten cents; five for the paper, five for the "sir," perhaps.

As we move toward the subway entrance we pass the Café de l'Opéra, deserted, cold, and grey, and, thinking of the fall of Babylon, we shiver. It must be getting chilly. We started out to be amused. But, have we been?

"NO ADMITTANCE"

III

"NO ADMITTANCE"

IT is a battered little door tucked away, almost always, in a decayed side street or dingy court and sheltered by a flimsy wooden vestibule, as secretive and disreputable looking as the side entrance of a Raines-law hotel; and, like the Raines-law door, it usually sleeps idly through the day, but wakes to shadowy activity when night begins to fall. What you find at the stage door depends largely upon yourself, your business, and your point of view concerning the stage entrance of a theatre.

The guardian of the portal is a bulky misanthrope, combining the suspicious nature of a Russian frontier policeman with the bristling manner of the Jack-in-the-box that guarded the toy kingdom in the fairy tale. In every stranger who appears at the stage door, he sees either a process server with a summons for the star, a Pittsburg Lochinvar who has come out of the West to carry off a fairy princess, or a mere case of "touch"—in any case an undesirable alien.

When, on a recent occasion, the Artist and myself undertook to beard the doorman in his den, I told the Artist (who has a most persuasive manner) that he might do the talking. But it turned out that the doorman did most of it. . . . "Well, what d' y' want?" . . . "Well, he's busy." . . . "Well, what d' y' want to see 'im about?" . . . Meanwhile I pretended to be reading the dressing-room list, the boarding-house list, the rehearsal call, and the "No Admittance" and "No Smoking" signs, which are posted just inside the door of every theatre.

When, at last, we were admitted, the Artist rushed to the stage, snatched a gilded and

The Stage-door Man

beribboned three-legged milking stool from a gilded and beribboned two-legged milk-maid, dropped down upon it, and began to sketch—just to show he was sincere.

In these days of high-school fraternities and juvenile men of the world, the youngest of us all knows something of the seamy side of the theatrical curtain. Our sons inform us that New Haven, once a famous seat of learning, has latterly become a celebrated "dog town"; a place where "shows" are "tried out"—with all the implied educational advantages.

But for my part, I must confess that when I pass into the region which we call "behind the scenes" (referred to in the theatre as "back"), my attitude is not that of calm, cynical scrutiny. The bare brick walls, the iron stairways leading up to dress-ing-rooms; the shadowy, black fly-gallery, far above; the dusty, splintered boards be-neath my feet; the canvas side-scenes cov-ered with rude painting, or with the backs of books glued on in rows to make a library; above all, the inscrutable painted people waiting for their cues amid a litter of furniture, lighting apparatus, and "props," all combine to thrill me with the feeling that I have passed from the practical world into the warehouse of mystery and illusion.

Let the current of stage realism roar like a torrent over the footlights, not an ounce of it eddies into the backwaters of the wings. From the front the ordered drama may move with technical perfection toward its climax, but seen through a hole in the back drop, it becomes unconvincing and grotesque. That little peephole, so dear to the stage hands, is an opera-glass which sees Make-believe stalking upon the boards, a naked thing, brazen and absurd.

An actor whose age you cannot guess, through the wrinkles pencilled on his face and the white wig bulging over his hair, walks slowly off the stage. He is the father in the play. He comes and talks with you

LET THE CURRENT OF STAGE REALISM
ROAR, LIKE A TORRENT, OVER THE
FOOTLIGHTS, NOT AN OUNCE OF IT
EDDIES INTO THE BACKWATERS OF
THE WINGS

about the baseball scores.   Near by, a plank
and two sand-bags are dropped upon a quilt
stretched out upon the boards.   The sound
is that of a dead, crumpling fall.   A young
actor, beyond the canvas wall, shrieks
"Father!" and comes rushing off the scene.
Then he strolls over and shakes hands with
you, but, as he does so, turns his face stage-
ward and bellows: "Get the doctor!" Then
he joins calmly in the baseball talk.

Meanwhile there is agitated running on
and off.   A maid in cap and apron hurries
up a flight of stairs which, once out of view
of the audience, ends abruptly in mid-air.
At the top of the flight she waits long enough
to have ascended to a bedroom on a supposi-
titious second floor.   Then, taking up a
pillow, which the property man must put
there every night, she rushes down again,
seen briefly by the audience as she passes
the hall door.

And what does it all mean?

It means that poor old "father" (still

talking baseball with you) had an apoplectic stroke and fell upon the stairs. The
plank and sand-bags that they dropped
were "father." And, of course, the maid
ran up and got the pillow to ease "father's"
final moments. "Father" is dead, and the
first act is over. So, presently, when the
topic of baseball is exhausted (which it
quickly is with me) "father" says good-night
and hastens to his dressing-room, envied by
all the other members of the company.
From the front his stroke is tragedy. From
the back it is luck—a short part that lets
"father" leave the theatre in time to see the
latter half of all the other plays on Broadway. For it is a fact worth noting that few
lovers of the theatre see so little of it as
successful players.

Take your actor friend to dinner, or—if
you can get him to—let him take you. Talk
with him of current affairs—if you can keep
him from talking of himself. After dinner

"JACK" BARRYMORE

accompany him to the theatre in which he is comedian, hero, or villain. In his dressing-room he slips out of his street clothes, sits down before a mirror, and daubs his face with grease paint. Stroke by stroke, your friend disappears before your eyes, until, with the last touch, he is quite gone. He has become a painted picture.

"Make-up," said De Goncourt, "coarsens the skin, makes the muscles immovable, and does not permit the soul of the actor to pass through his plastered face." As your friend's soul leaves his face, it also leaves the conversation. You do not feel at home with this new, vague personality.

With actresses it is not quite the same. In conversing with an actress who is heavily made up, you (or should I say I?) become only slightly more absurd than when talking with a lady of the audience who wears a merely non-professional tint. The conversation takes the lady's hue. Paint is no thicker on the stage to-day than twenty years ago, but it is thicker in the parquet and the boxes. It is not the theatre, but the theatre-goer (which is to say, broadly, American society) that grows artificial. The actor and the actress are the only human beings who are paid for being other than the Creator made them; the rest of us are doing it for nothing.

The disappearance of your actor friend behind his mask of make-up is not only seeming. The costume is his business suit and the hour his business hour. Descend with him to the stage. Watch him go on for his scene with the woman star. See the suave way they play together, falling at last into each other's arms.

When the scene is over, your friend appears before you with a dramatic gesture of despair:

"You see what I'm up against!"

You don't see.

"My boy! Do you mean to say that

PAINT IS NO THICKER ON THE
STAGE TO-DAY, BUT IT IS
THICKER IN THE PARQUET
AND THE BOXES

you've not noticed how she kills my lines?
My laughs go for nothing! It's absurd to
call her an artist. Why, she absolutely hogs
everything!"

How often we see love scenes between an
actor and an actress who are not on speaking terms, or, worse, are on unpleasant
speaking terms. How often the sweet noth-
ings which the audience hears are like poi-
soned candies. I have known a star to seize
his leading woman's hand and, bending over
to imprint a lover-like kiss upon it, whisper:
"For Heaven's sake, why don't you clean
your nails?" . . . Oddly enough, he told me
that, himself!

If the actor does not see through his own
foibles, he at least views those of his profession with a keenly ironic eye. No stories
could be droller or more full of human character than an actor's stories about actors—
that one, for instance, about the handsome
leading man who opened a letter that con-

tained a tailor's dun, glanced through it, crumpled it up, and sighed: "Poor little girl!"

The egotism of the theatre is by no means confined to the players. If it originated with them it was contagious, for everybody in the playhouse has it now. The star is an egotist, the manager is an egotist, the leading woman and the leading man are egotists, the stage carpenter is an egotist, the property man is an egotist, the electrician is an egotist, the orchestra leader is particularly an egotist (which may account to some extent for the quality of theatre orchestras), the ushers are egotists, the box-office man, who tells you there are two left in the nineteenth row, is an egotist, and, to complete the list, the people who buy seats of him are egotists as well.

The "back stage" egotists are hungry for publicity.

"You're a writer, aren't you?" demands the electrician. "Here's a little piece I

IN ARCADY

wrote myself. You might use it in your paper. It tells all about theatre lighting. And say, mention my name—Cassidy."

Looking at the press sheet he has handed you, you discover that Mr. Cassidy has been indulging in the peculiar pastime of interviewing himself. His interview begins with the statement that "there is always something interesting about the theatre and theatrical affairs to the ordinary person." Being a very ordinary person, you read on and presently find out that the most interesting of all "the interesting things about the theatre and theatrical affairs" is Mr. Cassidy.

You escape from Mr. Cassidy and go to the star's dressing-room. He gives you a cigarette and has his dresser shut the door so that the fireman won't smell the smoke. Then he shows you a stack of letters on his dressing-table. It is the matinée idol's daily crop.

"Yes, you'll see a crowd of girls outside

the stage door after the performance. . . . They follow me to my hotel. . . . You'd be surprised to see how ladylike some of them look. . . . There was one . . . a charming little thing, too. Her father was one of the biggest men on the Dubuque Board of Trade. . . . She was fairly mad about me. . . . Ah, well! . . . I gave her some good advice and sent her home."

His "entrance music" sounds. He rises from his chair, throws his cloak over one shoulder with a dramatic gesture, and stalks onto the stage. As you watch him go you are touched upon the arm. It is the stage-manager.

"Be around at the end of the second act," he says, "and I'll show you something."

At the end of the second act you are accordingly "around."

"Nobody's got an idea how much I have to do with his success," the stage-manager declares, as you look out between the wings at the scene in the courtyard of the inn,

An Echo of "Floradora"

which nears its thrilling climax. "Just wait a minute. You'll see."

A moment later the big fight scene is on. The star's invincible rapier vanquishes, singly, a host of villains, piercing their astral bodies. The curtain drops. There is a burst of applause, sounding from the stage, like heavy rain upon a roof.

"He likes to make curtain speeches," says the stage-manager, ringing up the curtain for the encore, "but *I'm* the one that really gets the calls for him. For instance, that's what we call a 'quick curtain'; it teases the bunch out there."

Indeed, it seems to "tease" them, for the applause redoubles.

Again the quick curtain, this time revealing star and leading woman.

When this has been repeated several times, the applause diminishes. The wily stage-manager now leaves the curtain down for a long moment, but does not shut off the footlights nor illuminate the auditorium.

The audience consequently remains seated and expectant.

"Watch this," he says, with a wink, as he seizes the edge of the curtain and shakes it gently. Instantly the hands begin to clap again. The people out in front have seen the movement of the drapery and jumped to the conclusion that the star is coming out, alone, to bow. And they are very, very right. He appears, and with one hand on his heaving chest, and the other on the crimson curtain back of him, bows low, and exits quickly. This also is repeated several times —including curtain shaking.

"That's about all they'll stand," says the stage-manager at last. The star, it seems, is of the same opinion, for this time he does not withdraw so quickly but, after bowing, pauses. There is a deprecating smile upon his face, which seems to say: "Well, since you *insist*—" The house goes silent in an instant. There follows a moment in which the star seems to collect his thoughts. Then he makes his speech—the little speech that he has made a thousand or two times before: some flower of thought, as I recall it, about "thanking you one and all."

It is over in an instant. The stage-manager touches a button; the footlights are turned off, the house lights on. Stage-hands are already setting the scene for the third act, incidentally menacing your life by shooting canvas rocks upon you at express train speed and dropping painted forests on your head.

"Of course, the whole play came out of my novel," says the author of whichever of the six best sellers the play was taken from. (He is one of the great brood of literary Hopes raised by the author of "The Prisoner of Zenda.") "It's really my dramatisation that gets the applause," thinks the dramatist. "Confidentially, it's all my acting," says the star. "It's my beauty," says the leading woman, glancing at her mirror. "It's my tricks," the stage-manager assures you. "It's our applause," the audience cajoles itself as it gets into its limousine. And as the ushers make their final hunt beneath the seats for the nightly crop of jewellery, handkerchiefs, and gloves they doubtless say among themselves, "We done it."

A certain friend of mine is forever charging me with uttering generalities. But what is one to do? To call players fascinating, emotional egotists, to declare them hardworking, underpaid, ambitious, is to generalise. To say that all men have two legs is to generalise—and, incidentally, to do injustice to the flourishing industry of amputation. There is something about the stage, and also about legs, that induces generalities. Both, for example, are sometimes called immoral. Dumas the younger called the playhouse an immoral house, and Mr. Anthony Comstock and Mr. Florence Ziegfeld seem to be united in their opinion as to the immorality of legs—though it is but fair to add that the belief leads them into widely different fields of action.

Every one should know, by this time, that there are very moral stages, and every one does know that there are ridiculously moral legs. I have some rather deep convictions about both. I believe that the ballet dancer may be, and usually is, a spectacle as moral as a decoration on a Christmas tree. An ogling show girl in long skirts, prancing up and down before the footlights to the accompaniment of cheap music, may, on the other hand, be funny, vulgar, or immoral, as you look at it. She is a horrible reality, like so much raw beef. But the ballet dancer, flying through the air, with her twinkling pink legs and pointed toes, her gauze skirts and her eternal smile is, from the front, the most unreal of all the theatre's unrealities. She is no more real than an elaborate doll that is put away each night in a box with sachets and pink tissue paper.

I shall never forget an evening on which

we watched the Russian dancers, Mordkin and Pavlowa, from the wings of the Metropolitan Opera House. The last act of a spectacular German opera was in progress as we reached the mammoth stage. Through mysterious semi-darkness, full of moving figures, we worked our slow way to the wings. Green and blue footlights cast a dim, uncanny light upon the stage, set to represent a dank and rocky glen, in which raged a storm of supernatural fury. Thunder rolled—rolled literally, in the form of wooden balls that tumbled down a chute. The wind machine howled horribly. A thunderbolt slid down a wire and hissed out in a pail of water. Bats and will-o'-the-wisps flitted at the ends of wires, strange beasts crawled, gongs tolled, chains clanked, the orchestra gave forth melancholy waves of sound, and owls flapped their wings as a group of chorus women, just off the stage, gave voice to the wailing cry, "Whoo-ee! Whoo-ee!"

MORDKIN AND PAVLOWA

The storm was terrible, but brief. As its distant thunder died off among the painted hills, the full moon rose slowly, on its wire, in the peaceful sky of the back drop. Its soft electric light fell like a benediction on the canvas glen, and shimmered on a waterfall, behind which an industrious young man in a soiled sweater revolved an electric light cylinder. And as the peace of highly artificial night descended over all the world of calcium and canvas, the opera reached its end.

Like the flights of brilliant insects that appear after a tempest, the *ballerinas* now came flitting to the stage. From somewhere—beyond the great curtain or under the stage—came the medley of muffled sound that indicates a tuning orchestra. Violins shrilled brief, dissonant frivolities to their relatives, the bass viols and 'cellos, which replied in deprecating, serious tones. Flutes laughed in droll chromatic runs, kettledrums uttered rumbling chuckles, low-

pitched wind-instruments brayed sardonic-
ally, even a harp rippled, as a sweet-voiced
woman laughs behind her fan. I love to
hear a great orchestra tune up. It always
sounds to me as though the instruments
were whispering the gossip of the hour and
making bantering remarks to one another,
before settling down to work. It is a sound
full of promise, and it always fills me with
a delightful sense of expectancy.

As the tuning ceased, the *ballerinas,* after
rubbing their flat, stiff-soled slippers in resin
boxes, ranged themselves in rows upon the
stage, now set with a sweet woodland scene.
Then all eyes turned toward the wings,
where the two Russians appeared, moving
with easy, sinuous grace. Even in walking
they were beautiful to watch. I was struck
at once by the fact that both were below the
average in height, though from the front I
had received a quite opposite impression.

Of course, the matter of stature in the
theatre is purely relative. Size is one of the

most important factors in the engaging of a company. The little star wants pygmy players to surround him. A tall leading woman, however beautiful and talented, would make him look ridiculous in a romantic scene. I think it is Paul Wilstach who, in his book on the late Richard Mansfield, tells of the built-up boots, the illusory attitudes, and the cunningly scaled down furniture which that actor utilised to make himself look larger. I do not know whether *ballerinas* always come in tiny packages, or not, but those surrounding Mordkin and Pavlowa were all so small as to make the Russians look quite large by contrast.

Almost simultaneously with the arrival of the famous pair upon the stage, the overture struck up. The *ballerinas* assumed attitudes. Then, with a hissing sweep, the curtain rose. It was like the bursting of a dam. A torrent of music and of brilliant light rushed in, snatched the little *ballerinas,* and swirled them madly in its maelstrom.

And at the very centre of it all, like a pair of iridescent bubbles cast up by the flood, floated Mordkin and Pavlowa.

My doll fancy departed as I saw them dance. I could see their steel muscles gather for each bound, and hear the heavy thud of their toes upon the rough boards, after each soaring flight. Sometimes, as they flew by my hiding place, I even heard a quick-snatched breath.

When it was over Pavlowa was tired. All elasticity seemed to have gone from her slender little body. She walked slowly to the stairway leading upward to her dressing-room. Despite her fatigue I half expected her to give a leap and float up to the top step; but she did not. She paused wearily at the bottom of the flight. Then Mordkin came, and, taking one of her hands, went up ahead, tugging, while Pavlowa trudged after, drooping and flat-footed in her finery —a picture both pathetic and grotesque.

Apropos of this, it is worth mentioning

that in the Century Theatre players are not forced to walk up-stairs. One very practical way to "elevate the stage," it seems to me, is to elevate the actor in an elevator.

Another way might be to elevate the taste of the audiences.

The audience can make the theatre what it wills, but the theatre cannot make the audience. If we have vulgar "shows," it is because we have vulgar people to attend them. If we have vulgar "comedians," it is because we have vulgar pleasure-seekers to applaud them. It is so easy to be vulgar! You needn't even try—just let yourself go. What is the thing they call a "typical Broadway show" but one group of vulgar people who get upon a stage and let themselves go before another group of vulgar people? A vulgar librettist (who, before the days of "musical shows," would probably have found a place in life as a writer of rhymes in praise of soups or breakfast foods) lets himself go, and naturally produces maudlin ditties, rhyming "love" with "turtle dove." A vulgar composer then makes up a set of tra-la-la tunes, reminiscent of last season's crop. A vulgar manager engages a vulgar company and, after rehearsals by a vulgar stage manager, the vulgar show is ready for a vulgar audience. Isn't it simple? Isn't it easier than to create and put upon the stage clever, clean-cut comic operas, which are so rare?

And why trouble to be intelligent if people don't demand it of you? Why write a witty libretto, why compose good music, why engage legitimate comedians or good singers when people seem content without them? You know as well as I do what will make an American audience roar with laughter. It likes men in red whiskers to sing Irish songs. It likes men in plaid waistcoats stuffed with pillows, to splutter salivary German dialect into each other's faces. It likes fat women and fat men in little round hats, and it wants them to fall down while the drummer bangs his drum, and a stage-

THERE MUST BE A HEROINE
TO SING LOVE SONGS

hand drops the crash-box, in the wings. Then there must be a sort of hero and a sort of heroine to sing love songs, and there must be girls, girls, girls. Perhaps I should have mentioned the girls first.

From a strictly back-stage standpoint, the musical show is the most colourful and picturesque. The orchestra is forever strumming out gay tunes, the people are forever running back and forth in costumes pretty or comic, rushing on singly or in groups to sing or dance, then off again and up the iron stairs, to dressing-rooms, and other dresses. The air vibrates with life, light, and colour.

Despite the fact that celebrated actors of the legitimate stage—among them Jefferson and Mansfield—have risen from the chorus, a gap separates the people of the musical stage from those of the "legit." They are like different tribes of the same race, and they mingle to no great extent. The atmosphere, back stage, is not at all the same. The musical stage, while not invariably so, is generally more free and easy. Christian names—or perhaps I should say Christian stage names—are tossed freely back and forth:

"Say, Goldie, come over with my rouge pot."

"Aw, forget it, Beatrice. I ain't see' it."

If, instead of Goldie and Beatrice, they elaborately call each other "Miss Wentworth" and "Miss St. Clair," there is no indication of respect implied. On the contrary, it means a feud; and when the bad blood of those fine old families, the Wentworths and the St. Clairs of musical comedy, is aroused, one had better stand aside; for, even if nothing else is thrown, there is certain to be "langwidge."

For magnificence, only negro names can rival those of chorus girls. They take them whence they please. Neither society, finance, nor literature is safe from their pillaging researches. The chorus has its Vanderbilts, its Astors, its Belmonts, not to

JAMES MONTGOMERY FLAGG

WE LIKE FAT MEN IN
LITTLE ROUND HATS

mention its Montagues and Capulets. I remember one girl with masses of red hair who was known as Zaza Belasco, and another, with, perhaps, a penchant for jewellery, who was called Diamond Donner.* The names of the young women who figure in the programme under the headings: "Typewriter Girls, Tennis Girls, Summer Girls" are only too often funnier than the libretto.

The styles in women for these shows change like the styles in clothing. Where is the spear-carrying "Amazon" of yesteryear? Has she become extinct, or evolutionised by banting? Where is the tall, slender London "Gaiety Girl"? London doesn't want her any more. It now requires slender young girls whom it designates as "flappers."

Girls for the Broadway musical show of to-day come in sizes like the three bears in the children's story. There is the "great big" show girl, the "medium-sized" chorus

* Truth is stranger than musical comedy! Someone writes me that this is her real name!

girl, and the "little bit of a wee, wee" dancer.

Owing partly to uniformities of form and costume, partly to the heavy masks of make-up, and partly, perhaps, to other and more subtle likenesses, these girls seem, at close range, to resolve themselves into three types which are duplicated over and over as by a mould. You feel that you could hold a conversation with one show girl and, when she went on to represent a lady at the races, continue it with any of the others, without a seeming break.

About the chorus girls and the dancers you feel the same. They are simply scaled down from the show girls in size and, I fancy in "prosperity." The girl whom we saw working at embroidery behind the scenes was a chorus girl. So was the one who read Rousseau. So was the one who had been in the chorus of the Metropolitan Opera and wanted to go into vaudeville so that she and her young actor husband might be more together. But none of these was really true to type. They didn't even look so, and I like to fancy that their destinies are not the same as those of girls out of the mould.

But for the rest—Who are they, where do they come from, and why? The press agent has data of a not too satisfactory kind. Four of the eighty-eight girls in one representative company were graduates of women's colleges—so it was said. Sixteen had attended colleges, but had not graduated. Twenty-seven were high-school graduates, thirty-one had finished grammar school, and ten left school young to go to work. Eight were married, and all loved to "see their pictures in the paper," excepting one who didn't want her mother to find out that she was on the stage. Only seven of the eighty-eight were born in the city of New York; thirty-two were foreign-born, and the remaining forty-nine hailed from twenty-three states. Their ages ranged from seventeen to twenty-nine, sixty per cent. of them being under twenty-three.

The remaining statistics were principally concerned with heights, weights, colourings, and measurements, and seem too bare to bear upon this article——except that they show the point of view regarding chorus women. They are matched as horses are matched, and are valuable as horses are valuable: for reliability, endurance, good looks, and stylish action.

The statistics concerning education among the chorus girls surprised me. I am sure that I have never talked with one of them who went to college, though I have met several who gave every sign of having left school at a very, very early age; as, for example, the one who asked me at the time of the Cook-Peary controversy: "What's this North Pole that they're all the time talking about? Have they got a town up there?"

There is a kind of show girl—the "typical Broadway show girl," they call her—who

THEY ARE VALUABLE AS HORSES
ARE VALUABLE: FOR RELIABILITY,
ENDURANCE, GOOD-LOOKS AND
STYLISH ACTION

has, along the Great White Way, an odd sort of celebrity. She is seen about the restaurants, every night, with men who are conspicuous socially, financially, or drunkenly. Your Broadway mentor points her out to you as "the girl who got all the money out of young So-and-so," or "the girl who caused the What's-their-name's divorce." It seems from what he tells you that neither So-and-so nor What's-his-name had much to do with it. It was the woman; she tempted him and he did eat. It was, as the newspapers would say, an "actress"; a woman following what Birrell, in his "Obiter Dicta," calls "the only profession commanding fame and fortune the kind consideration of man has left open to her."

"For two centuries," says Birrell, "women have been free to follow this profession, onerous and exacting though it be, and by doing so have won the rapturous admiration of men, who are all ready to believe that where their pleasure is involved, no risks of life or honour are too great for a woman to run."

Unless it be the women of that smart society which they ape and envy, I suppose there is no class of women in the world so morbidly mundane, so super-sophisticated as these "successful" show girls, surrounded, as they are, by shams, false values, sordidness. They have their following, know why they have it, and how to make what seems to them the most of it.

There was in New York a year or two ago a show called "Girlies." It was advertised by the manager responsible for it with the catch line: "None of them married; none of them twenty."

Can you not see a Turkish slave dealer with a caravan of women going to market with that exultant cry?

Girlies—none of them married, none of them twenty! None of them protected! None of them old in the ways of the world!

Poor girlies! Those are the pitiful qualifications with which you are turned loose to make a living in that plague-spot of the world, Broadway!

Singing and prancing through your evenings in the theatre, seeing the "prosperity" of some of your fellow "girlies" and knowing whence it comes, where do you go when, after the performance, you pass out through the dingy little door? Do you scurry home alone to your hall bedroom? Or do you go to meet "Prosperity"—Prosperity in evening dress—awaiting you, out there beneath the shadows of the street lamp?

Poor girlies!

But there was one of you who gave the lie to that insinuating catch-line. Yes, one of you was married, and the whole world of Broadway found it out one morning when it read its papers. That "girlie" was the one whose husband waited for her, in the dark, outside the little door, chased her through the New York streets, and shot her.

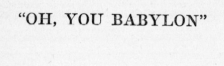
"OH, YOU BABYLON"

IV

"OH, YOU BABYLON!"

"I can see that you are married,
    And you know I'm married, too,
And nobody knows that you know me,
    And nobody knows that I know you . . ."

HIPS, arms, and head a-swinging with her song, hands flipping up and down like fins, the girl with the oakum hair moved before the tables in a lazy, undulating shuffle suggesting a mermaid swimming in tobacco smoke. Her mouth was open wide—a large, red-painted bull's-eye in the round white target of her face—but the sounds emitted lacked the allurement of a Rhine maiden's song. They were, rather, a Rhine-wine maiden's nasal notes.

The people at the tables hedging in the open space in which she gyrated to the rag-time music of the little orchestra, observed her with varying degrees of interest. A tall, aristocratic woman in a black evening gown looked stiffly through her lorgnon, as who should say: "Let me hear and see, and get it over with." To three other women, sitting with their escorts at the next table, the cabaret was clearly an old story. They wore Broadway faces and Fifth Avenue toilettes—gowns too fine, faces not fine enough. Resting bare, creamy elbows on the dead-white cloth, they presented to the singers three pairs of eyes like those of lazy, purring Sphinxes, and to the spectators, ranged at remoter tables in the rear, three glorious white backs, each, as it were, endeavouring to outstrip the other in the acuteness of its "eternal triangle." Now and then one of them lifted to her lips a champagne glass or a cigarette, taking a light draught from the one or a deep draught from the other.

"Her voice," remarked one of the escorts,

There Is Little That Is Funny, Much That Is Revolting, in the Folly of a White-haired Man

"is slightly corked." Fondling a half-foot amber cigarette-holder, he cast sad eyes upon the singer.

"Put on another record," rejoined another.

Save for minor differences (such as the initials on their cigarettes and the names on their visiting cards) the three young men were as like as three young dandies in a shirt and collar advertising lithograph. They were fashionable, night-prowling New Yorkers, clean-cut as to hair and clothing, polished as to finger-nails.

Having passed their table and sung a second verse, the girl was once more shrilling the chorus. She had stopped dancing, and was leaning with one hand on a table at which sat three old men, dapper and delighted.

"I can see that you are married   .   .   ."

The three exchanged significant glances and giggled foolishly together, while people at the other tables sneered and snickered. There is little that is funny, much that is revolting, in the folly of a white-haired man. It chills the blood—even hot, young blood—and causes youth to wonder, horrified: Will I ever come to be like that? But cabaret girls must make people laugh. Still singing her refrain, the girl leaned farther over the table, thrusting her pert, ill-shaped nose closer and closer to that of the *vieillard* facing her. In the mocking stare of her cold, glittering eyes there was something of the reptile; in the blank, blinking look he gave her back, something of the reptile's prey—of the helpless toad, terrified yet charmed. Closer came the cruel eyes. A silly smile was frozen on his lips.

". . . If you care to, we'll have luncheon,
Every day, here, just the same;
But swee-tart . . ."

Her bare, whitened arm shot out; her fingers tickled him beneath the chin, in a derisive caress which was like the strike of a snake:

THREE GLORIOUS WHITE BACKS,
EACH ENDEAVORING TO OUTSTRIP
THE OTHER IN THE ACUTENESS
OF ITS "ETERNAL TRIANGLE"

". . . if you talk in your sleep,
   Don't men-shun my name!"

With the final word she turned abruptly and cast a crimson smile about the room. People applauded her and laughed, as they will at brazen youth. With a sort of start the old man she had baited came to life— or to something as like life as there was left in him. He felt a feeble but insistent impulse to hold up his non-existent end of the non-existent joke; to "come back," as they say on Broadway. So he cackled, clapped his hands, and called upon the girl to sit down at his table. But she had done with him. Without so much as looking around, she moved away.

A certain Broadway sentimentalist I wot of, could take, as a beginning, a scene something like this, and make from it a pretty romance. I can see what he would do. He would roll the episode in the sugar of his imagination, and place upon its apex the candied fruit of final happiness. In his

story the old man would not be a fool, but
a fine old figure, a millionaire, with a house
on Fifth Avenue and a heartache. (You
see, he had a daughter once, who etc., etc.
She would have been just the age of this
girl had she but etc. etc.)

As for the cabaret girl in the story, she
would have a "strange air of refinement."
It would puzzle you until it was disclosed
that she came of "a fine old Southern family." Little do her poor old mother and
lame sister, at home, know how she earns
the money to support them! But the
shrewd eye of the old millionaire (and, now
that I think of it, my friend the sentimentalist would make him a Colonel with a
white goatee) would quickly fathom the fic-
tional fact that this girl was "not like the
rest." He would call her to his table and
talk with her in "low, well-bred tones,"
while about them all was smoke and rev-
elry. He would ask about her past. She
would tell him her real name.

Then, to his surprise, and hers——and ours—?——the truth would be revealed! The girl would be his niece—the daughter of his scapegrace brother, long since dead! Together they would rise from the table, the bent old man and the fair young girl. Out in the night, beyond the gilded portals of the cabaret, would be standing the colonel's "perfectly appointed brougham." A "trim footman" would open the door. The colonel would "hand the girl in" ahead of him. Then, as she "dropped back upon the soft cushions," symbolic of the luxurious future awaiting her as his adopted daughter, the colonel would turn to his footman and pronounce the single, significant word "Home!"—which would end the story.

As he wrote that final word, I think my Broadway sentimentalist would drop a tear upon his manuscript. I am sure that he cries over his stories after a certain point, just as he cries over his high balls after a certain hour. And for my part I could almost cry over his stories myself.

Alas for romance! No such story was enacted. As the real cabaret girl, in all her panoply of unreality, left him, the real old man felt not at all paternal. He was thinking, on the contrary, that the young girl had a pretty body, and that he was not so old, after all, as to be unattractive to "the ladies." Hadn't she picked him out to sing to? He threw out his chest and patted down the whisps of white hair upon his bald spot.

The cabaret girl's mind was countless centuries older than the rest of her. She knew that she had hypnotised him, as she had so many other old men, before. She always picked an old one for that sort of thing; the young ones "guy" back, sometimes, which is inconvenient. "Now that he's out of his trance," she said to herself, "I mustn't notice the old silly. When they're like that they want to pinch my arm, put their clammy

MORGAN

A Favourite

hands on my shoulder, and make me dance with them."

It was a manicure girl who first set me to wondering about cabarets. I had heard vague rumours that a wave of cabarets had broken on the Broadway coast, and had made a mental note of the fact, as one notes the abstract news that several million Chinese families are perishing from famine. Then there came an afternoon when I found myself indulging in the polite folly of having my nails "done," and the still greater folly of listening to the blond person's prattle of food and fashion.

"Well," she said, "I suppose you've been to that new restaurant at Broadway and Forty-eighth?"

"No," I admitted, looking idly at the buffer flying back and forth. "It's another cabaret, isn't it?"

"Oh, no," she replied. "A gentleman friend took me there the other night.

There's an orchestra and singers—no dancing."

"Does it take dancing, then," I asked, "to turn a restaurant into a cabaret?"

"Sure," she answered.

"What does the word cabaret mean?" I asked.

The shoulders, beneath her peekaboo waist, went up in an indifferent shrug.

"Search me," she said. "It's something new."

Clearly she was more interested in eating than in etymology, in filling than philology.

Presently she gave my hand that final tap which means "I've finished," and I placed in hers that final tip which is the answer, and departed.

It was spring—spring on Fifth Avenue. Buds were shooting in the milliners' windows; a soft haze of exhaust gases from automobiles filled the air and wafted like incense to the nostrils, while on every hand could be heard the soft low note of the motor honking to its mate.

Waiting to cross the street, I met a stock-broker I know, and to him repeated my inquiry concerning the word cabaret.

"I have it," he replied, "straight from Steve, the head bartender at Rector's. The word cabaret is a compound—like a cock-tail, you understand—made of two pure old Broadway words: 'cab'—a means of getting there, and 'hooray'—a noise made there."

I thanked him.

"Great time to buy stocks," he declared, a fiery glitter showing in his eye.

When a broker attempts business with a writer it is a sign that things are very, very dull in Wall Street.

"Good-bye," I said hurriedly, and turned into the nearest doorway.

The place proved to be the Public Library. Being, as I just said, a writer, I had never been inside a library before. I was about to rush out, when the sight of a stewdious-looking man reminded me again of cabarets. The very place! You can find out anything in a library. Within a quarter of an hour I had found the inquiry desk.

"I wish to know about cabarets," I said to the young man behind the desk.

"You have made an error," he replied, regarding me oddly, through his large, round glasses. "This is the Public Library. Broadway is two blocks west."

I explained further.

"Ah!" he said, "you'll find it in Larousse, on a shelf just inside the door of the next room."

I set off at once. Within ten or fifteen minutes I had reached the next room. Finding Larousse, I turned the pages, with shimmering finger-nails, until I came upon the word:

CABARET: Tavern, bar, or little inn; house where one sells drinks in detail, or where one gives also to eat.

I read on. Nothing about singing and dancing; nothing about evening dress. As for the "newness" of the cabaret, three hundred years ago a poor Parisian poet wrote an "Ode to all the Cabarets of Paris." The famous cabarets at that time were the Sucking Calf, the Valley of Misery, and the Pomme de Pin, or Pine-cone. The last-named, though long since torn down, is famous to this day as having been the resort of him whom Stevenson called "the sorriest figure on the rolls of fame," the poet François Villon. Rabelais, too, patronised the Pomme de Pin; "indeed (says Larousse) the place was the haunt of those poets and rhymsters who opened the seventeenth century with the noise of their glasses and their songs."

As time went by, many of the old cabarets of Paris disappeared, while a few elevated themselves, by virtue of good cuisine and wines, to the rank of first-class restaurants. Among the latter may be mentioned

Voisin's and the Café Anglais, where monarchs, visiting in Paris, dine to-day.

In the Bohemian region of Montmartre the cabaret underwent another sort of evolution—an evolution from which sprang the current Broadway idea that cabaret means entertainment. Here there came into being certain small establishments, half cheap café, half club, known as *cabarets artistiques,* where met those strange, dirty, clever, shock-headed, slouch-hatted eccentrics who belong especially to Paris and stand, the world over, as the ultimate of the type Bohemian. Originally, these *cabarets artistiques* were not open to the public, but were held sacred to the Montmartre poets, minstrels, and ballad-mongers. But presently the echoes of their songs percolated through closed shutters to the streets and aroused a curiosity which ended in invasion. As sightseers came in, the flame of genuine Bohemianism went out, and the

HEAD-WAITER
A CABARET

cabaret artistique, becoming commercialised, presently expired.

Not so, however, the entertainment idea. Certain small, peculiar theatres, existing in Montmartre to-day (the Boîte au Fursy, the Grand Guignol, etc.), are outgrowths of the *cabaret artistique,* as are also the innumerable *cafés concerts* and the all-night restaurants in which paid singers and dancers perform between the tables.   It is from these Parisian supper places that New York has taken its conception of the cabaret.   But for all that, the word still holds in France its old primary significance of cheapness and inferiority: *dîner de cabaret,* implying a bad dinner, and *vin de cabaret,* bad wine.

When one speaks of Broadway, one does not think of the steamship offices in the canyon of lower Broadway; the wholesale shirt, cloak and suit, feather and umbrella district above City Hall Park; the old department stores between Union and Madison Squares; but of that strange, sordid mile-and-a-half which is given over to amusement, and which—with its unimportant buildings and its general cheap look, only partially redeemed by an occasional fine hotel—must be a bitter disappointment to those who, having heard George M. Cohan's patriotic songs about it, see the street for the first time.

Yet it has interesting features: It is the hottest, tawdriest street on earth at midday in the summer; the coldest, cruelest street at midnight in the winter; and if inhabitants of other planets, gazing at us through their telescopes, see brilliant flashes in the night and think that we are signalling to them, it is because commercial gentlemen with goods to sell are signalling, not upward to the heavens, but downward to the earth. For the rest, what does Broadway offer us? Theatres named for other theatres in the European capitals; European actors playing European plays in European clothing; restaurants called after famous Paris eating-places; French cooking, French cooks, French waiters, and French wines.

So far as our restaurants are concerned, the French invasion is not to be deplored. No one who is civilised, or even semi-civilised, will mourn the loss of the "strictly American" restaurant which flourished in such numbers upon Broadway until a decade or so since. Gone are its checker-board marble floors, its heavy, plush-upholstered chairs, its armoured plates and side-dishes, its Irish waiters (seasoning the soup with their thumbs), its unimaginative, uninviting bills of fare, set in type once for all, when the establishment first opened, and never changed save when a dish or two was added in peculiar purple handwriting. Why, I wonder, were all those ancient bills of fare written in purple and in the same illegible hand? It is one of the unsolved problems of our unlovely gastronomic past. Suffice it that the eating-house of other days has gone to an unhonoured grave in its own greasy gravy.

Even in New York the cabaret is not so new as many manicures and taxi-drivers suppose. Six or eight years since, many well-known artists frequented the Cabaret Francis in Thirty-fifth Street. Almost as long ago there was a "cabaret show" at the gay old Café Boulevard (which has a good one still) in Second Avenue. "Cap" Churchill, proprietor of the Broadway restaurant which bears his name, gives the cabaret an even longer local lineage, harking back to Billy McGlory's and other dives that antedate the days of Lexow. When I spoke to him upon the subject, the "Cap" (though he runs one now) set his face sternly against cabarets. At that time he entertained his patrons with a concert.

"They'll 'can' this cabaret stuff," he remarked. "It's just 'joint' stuff."

"MY ROSARY . . . MY ROSARY!"

There is truth in the diagnosis. The "joints" may fairly claim a sort of cousinship with this new-come French jade: the sort of cousinship there is between the woman of the streets and the favourite of a king. Things change. It takes time to "educate" the public. Moe would not go to the "joints," so the "joints" are brought to Moe. Besides, he'll tell you, cabarets are altogether different. They cost more. The women are "dolled up" and the walls are gilt. The "joints," upon the other hand, were dim and dismal. You went to them by narrow stairs that seemed to lead to Hades. Tough waiters brought bad whiskey, and bawled songs, like "The Rosary," in equally bad whiskey voices, while a "professor" banged on a piano which was steeped in beer and stuffed with cigarette butts.

Ah, gentle reader! it is hard to realise that Music, heavenly maid, is still young in the big Broadway restaurants! Her life, though brief, has been so full!   But a decade since, combined with potted palms, she could impart to any Broadway café a rakish and clandestine flavour!   Consider her to-day. We hear her screaming everywhere.   We masticate our morning egg to rag-time, lunch and dine to the strains of the pseudo-passionate waltz, and, after the theatre (where, doubtless, we ran into something called a "cabaret show") sup like Oriental potentates, amid the minstrelsy and dancing of the neurotic, exotic, tommy-rotic cabaret.

Tenderloin etiquette gives the Forty-second-Street-French pronunciation to the name of Louis Martin, calling it "Looey Mar-*tan*," and thus separating in one's mind the Martin family of Broadway, which feeds one on food, and the Martin family of Fifth Avenue which, represented by Frederick Townsend Martin, feeds one on beautiful thoughts.

Entering the glittering establishment of

We Sup, Like Oriental
Potentates, Amid the
Minstrelsy and Dancing
of the Neurotic, Exotic
Tommy-rotic Cabaret

Louis Martin, you see (as you look over the heads of the "hat-snatchers" who wrest your outer garments from you) the ground-floor restaurant in all the splendour of its barbaric black and blue and gold. An orchestra is playing; people are supping; a gay scene you'd have called it before the invention of the cabaret. But now! . . . Poor innocents! Sunday-school picknickers! . . . With a hollow, mocking laugh, you move toward the lift. To the head waiter, who intercepts you, you whisper your name. A glance at his list and he stands aside. You step into the car. The door slides shut behind you. You have disappeared, mysteriously, like the man in the trick cabinet; your body, and along with it whatever soul you may have, is being wafted upward, like the spirit of a good Mohammedan, to a paradise where houris dance.

There is an artificial air of secrecy and sin about it all. You have (unless you are too jaded to have feelings any more) the delightful sensation of doing something you ought not to do, back of which is the comfortable consciousness that the sin is only seeming. Still, the fact that you get in proves that you have a clean shirt and a solvent appearance; that, in the eyes of a head waiter, careful as a bank cashier, you look like the very devil of a fellow, take you buy and large.

The room upon which the elevator disgorges you, carries out the fancy of a Mohammedan paradise. It is "as Oriental as a rug" or as the harem scene from Sumurûn. Three walls are of gold; the fourth is faced with mirrors, giving an illusory effect of double space and double crowd. Nor are the people reflected only in the glasses. Despite variety of colour in costume and complexion, they are as like as a line of taxicabs.

Now and then you read in the Sunday supplement of a race of head-hunters or

pygmies, discovered in their forest fast-
nesses by some intrepid explorer who likes
to print "F. R. G. S." after his name. The
Artist and I, however, don't go in for that
sort of exploring. It disarranges the clothing and—as the young Briton remarked of
the theatre—"cuts into one's evenings so."
Instead of discovering new races in darkest
Africa, therefore, we gum-shoe after them
in lightest New York, after dark. Hence
this cabaretting.

We call our new-found race the Hectics.
Manhattan is their habitat. They first
made their appearance in considerable numbers at about the time the appendicitis op-
eration became general (though we at-
tach no special significance to the fact).
Their numbers are rapidly increasing, as
they breed in those alcoholically damp
places which are found in such abundance
in New York. In colouring, both males and
females run to shades of red; the males getting theirs through the application of alcohol

within and hot barber-shop towels without;
the females theirs from paint.

They do not paint in stripes, but rather
in spots, after the manner of the ancient
sisterhood of Cyprians. In the matter of
trappings they also emulate the courtesan;
they are not so much women wearing
clothes, as clothes containing women. In
their light, tight walking-skirts or their al-
luring evening gowns, their clothing cries
so loud of sex that one may be forgiven if
one wonders whether Robert W. Chambers
hasn't dropped his pen and gone to cutting
paper dress-patterns.

You may see them on Fifth Avenue by
day, or by night in the famous feeding-
places where, in combination with the
Broadway "regulars" and the visiting "vol-
unteers," the Hectics keep the golden
ball a-rolling. For the rest, their tribal
game is bridge and their tribal dance the
turkey-trot—executed to the tune of their
national hymn, which Franklin P. Adams

"Hectics"

has super-named "Everybody's Overdoing It." The female Hectic may readily be recognised by a sort of beauty that she has— the carnal beauty of loose, red lips, of feverish eyes, shining from the shadows of her low-piled hair, like those of some wild beast, gazing from a cave, at night. The male travels with her. He has a golden cigarette case, she a gold mesh-bag; receptacles in which, it is believed, they carry their ideals.

As you pass to your little table in Louis Martin's cabaret, your dress coat brushes several sorts of scented talcum from the backs of several fillies of the Tenderloin. You seat yourself, and after deciding between champagne and high-balls (at forty cents apiece) begin to look about. Perhaps you see at other tables, men you know. Perhaps the women with them are their wives—some wives *do* look like that, nowadays, remember. But let us not pursue this line of inquiry too far. Let us rather heed the admonition of the Etiquette Department of the *Morning Telegraph*—the *Ladies' Home Journal* of the Tenderloin—which warns us that it is not good form (dealing in round figures) to notice with whom our friends may happen to be, in cabarets.

The room is packed with little tables, valuable according to their proximity to the open space left at the centre for the performers; the space in which we have already seen the nasal singer baiting an old man.

Now comes a little Spanish girl with jet-black hair and eyes, and castanets in her white hands. She is young—youth is at a premium in cabarets—and she dances well, revolving like a top in her spangled, springy skirt, now bending backward like a willow in the wind, now stamping her small heels and posturing as proudly as a matador. Fela Hidalgo, she is called. She has danced earlier this evening in a Broadway theatre. And in her tireless dancing is another story for the sentimental fictionist.

SHE IS YOUNG—YOUTH IS AT
A PREMIUM IN CABARETS

Having made some reputation as dancers at the *Cirque de Paris* in Madrid, Fela and her brother came last year to New York, and soon found an engagement at Louis Martin's. They had been here but a short time, however, when the brother developed tuberculosis. Since then, Fela has been dancing for both. Her brother is in the country near Marseilles. They think that he is getting better. And there you have another plot. *Ohé!* I wish I had the magic wand of Merlin (or, failing that, the magic "wad" of Mr. Carnegie) with which to touch Hidalgo's little heels; for if I had, each stamping of them would mint golden coins upon the carpet.

Cabaret nights are long. Other dancers, other singers come; fillers-in, just good enough to please an easily contented audience, which, with stomach and palate purring pleasantly, await Maurice.*

Maurice (the French pronunciation,

* Maurice has lately moved up town to Reisenweber's.

please!) is the king-pin of the cabaret, high priest of the decadent dance. He came from Paris, turkey-trotting on the crest of this all-engulfing wave of cabarets, was washed up Broadway, and has since been whirling madly in Louis Martin's maelstrom. Having introduced the *danse des Apaches* at the Café de Paris, Maurice arrived here as an international figure. He was more interviewed than an ambassador. There was a rumour that, in the violence of a dance, he had once (and once is enough) broken his woman partner's neck. Presently one heard that certain ladies, whose names are known to every clerk who reads the society columns, had actually put down their Pomeranians and cigarettes, taken up their skirts, and trod a measure with Maurice.

Societies opposed to what one might call the "Mauricent" school of dancing, got him to give exhibitions by way of showing them how shocked they ought to be. And the word went forth that of all tangos and all turkey-trots, of all sliding, gliding, twisting, swirling, wreathing, writhing, man-and-girling dances, these were most apt to appal the prude and please the prurient.

Mr. Charles Frohman, in a recent interview, was quoted as saying something to the effect that the two important theatrical discoveries of the past season were Maurice and Gaby Deslys—both from France, and both, in a manner of speaking, dancers. Gaby didn't dance in cabarets; indeed, she didn't dance much anywhere, though any one could see she did her best. For the rest, the lady (you pronounce it Gah-bee Day-leece, by the way) had strings of things that looked like pearls, a rather pretty figure, a certain *chic*, and the name of having been the "lady friend" (as they say on Broadway) of a certain little European king who lately lost his job. Personally, I think the story about Gaby and her little king is press-agent work, and much exag-

gerated.   I might even call it false, but for
the fear that Gaby, being a French *artiste*
and jealous of her reputation, might sue the
publisher and me for damages.

As for Maurice, he is a graceful, well-
built young man, debonair and cocksure in
his beautifully fitting evening dress.   Mischief dances in his fringed blue eye, and
something more than mischief hangs about
the corners of his cruel, complacent, full-
lipped mouth.   The little orchestra strikes
up a waltz.   Jaded Hectics indicate expectancy by sitting up and filling glasses.
Their shoulders fall into the rhythm, working up and down like the walking-beams of
old side-wheelers.   Several hundred more
or less astigmatic eyes focus, as best they
can, upon the end of the room at which
performers first appear.   Maurice steps
forward with his partner—a girl young and
blonde and dainty enough to lead a Senior
"Prom."

At first they waltz for all the world like

a pair of exceptionally good dancers at a ball. The tempo becomes more rapid. Suddenly the man flings the girl away from him violently, as a boy throws a top. Holding to his hand, she spins until their two arms are outstretched. Then, with a jerk, he draws her back again, revolving, to his arms. They have not missed, in step or gesture, the fraction of a beat in the well-marked measure. The time changes. Dancing in circles, the girl leans back upon his hand, as if it were a sort of couch. Then, facing one another, and dropping into still another step, they move sidewise in a straight line, down the room. Her face is turned upward; her gaze is buried in his eyes. It is a luminous gaze. She clings to him, her stride following his as naturally and swiftly as spoke follows spoke in a fast-flying wheel. More and more rapidly they dance. The eye of the onlooker becomes bewildered. It seems to see them stepping through each other, each body giving way before the other as if its substance were no more real than those light, transparent gauzes which the ancients called "woven air."   So they mingle and blend together—a black cloud and a moonbeam, tearing cyclonically through space in which the planets rock.

Then, of a sudden, the terpsichorean dream is shattered.   The moonbeam detaches herself and turns to girl, again. With a leap, she alights astride her partner's hips and, fastened to his waist with the hooks of her bent knees, swings outward and away from his whirling body like a floating sash.   It is the climax of the dance; not so ungraceful as it sounds, perhaps, and more astonishing.   Speed relieves much of its vulgarity, leaving it bizarre—the more bizarre because the dancers are in evening dress, instead of being habited as acrobats. It is incongruity, as much as grace, which makes Maurice's dances so effective.

A great many people will tell you that these dances are quite new; a great many

A BLACK CLOUD AND
A MOONBEAM, TEARING
CYCLONICALLY THROUGH
SPACE

others (remembering that Wallace Irwin mentioned the "bunny-hug" ten years ago in his "Love Sonnets of a Hoodlum") will say they came from San Francisco. The fact is, however, that all these turkey-trots, tangos, bunny-hugs, grizzly-bears, Texas-tommies, etc., are the illegitimate descendants of the old *valse chaloupé,* which has been danced for the past thirty years, and probably much longer, in the dives around Les Halles in Paris, and which, I believe, still forms a part of the quadrilles at the Bal Bullier. The *valse chaloupé* was doubtless taken to San Francisco by members of that city's French colony, and thus came to be adopted by the "Barbary Coast."

Almost every cabaret in New York has its Maurice. Shanley's new place, in Lobster Square—largest of Broadway cabarets —has had Jack Clifford and Irene Weston. Clifford used to be head waiter in a "joint" called Sweeney's; Irene, an habituée.

Sweeney's "joint" was so often thrown out by the police, that it finally was permanently dislocated, so to speak. And the wonder is that Irene's joints aren't dislocated too ⸺so violent is the dance she does with Clifford. Like other premier cabaret performers, they have "doubled" in a Broadway theatre, and even in Shanley's they dance upon a stage, and with a spot-light on them ⸺for Shanley's cabaret is almost like a music-hall.

The general run of singers and dancers in the cabarets, along Broadway, are much the same in one place as another. When I was last at Maxim's the *pièce de résistance* was the Apache dance, done extremely well by a couple dressed as a Paris tough and toughess. This dance, though sordid, has, to my mind, a redeeming histrionic quality which lifts it above dances that depend on acrobatics, or on sex, for their appeal. The performers must be actors quite as much as dancers, for the Apache dance has the rare

THE "APACHE" DANCE HAS
THE RARE DISTINCTION OF
POSSESSING PLOT

distinction of possessing plot. There is no allure about it—not even the charm of physical beauty set off by flashing silks—nothing which makes vice seem anything but horrible. Its action is direct and brutal; its music peculiarly sinister; and when you have seen it to the end, you turn away with a shudder, for you have witnessed a terpsichorean interpretation of the life of a "white slave."

One of the most peculiar and novel developments along the cabaret line was inaugurated by the brothers Bustanoby when they ran the Café des Beaux Arts. This was the opening of a completely equipped turkey-trotting department in a ballroom at the rear of the main restaurant. It was popular, and had a peculiar patronage, half Broadway, half Fifth Avenue. Dancing lasted late into the mornings. But something went wrong at the Beaux Arts, and the two brothers who had operated there got out, leaving the place to a third mem-

ber of the family who, I take it, was more
circumspect, for he abolished turkey-trotting, to the general sorrow of the Tenderloin élite.

The turkey-trotting brothers were, however, not to be circumvented. They opened
another restaurant—Bustanoby's—but a
few blocks distant, where dancing is per-
mitted, nay, abetted. George Rector's new
establishment, which is just above Fifty-
ninth Street, on the exact line that separates
the up-town and the down-town Tender-
loins, also installed an admirable turkey-
trotting plant, and Murray's Roman Gar-
den in Forty-second Street followed suit.
In the latter two establishments one may
sup on the ground floor in unblissful un-
consciousness of the rag-time, the swaying
shoulders, and the shuffling feet two floors
above. There is a long ballroom at George
Rector's, at one end of which are little tables
where a "Supper Tabarin" is served. And

"Everybody's Overdoing It"

of course those who come to trot remain to pay.

In mild weather Murray's supper-tables are spread upon a comfortable roof-garden, where turkey-trotters may combine the process of cooling off with that of putting provender where it belongs. And it is wonderful indeed to see how much a single little chorus girl can eat and drink, when food and liquor are laid in in layers, between the dances.

I feel apologetic. I have only scratched the surface of the cabarets—but that may be because the cabarets have naught save surfaces to scratch. From Little Hungary in Houston Street, to Pabst's vast armory-like restaurant in One-Hundred-and-Twenty-fifth, you will find them everywhere: rag-time, turkey-trotting spots upon the city map; gay cabarets, jay cabarets; cabarets with stages and spot-lights, cabarets without; cabarets on ground floors, in cellars, and on roofs; cabarets where "folks act gen'l'mumly," cabarets where the wild time grows.

Nor must you fancy you have reached the northern cabaret belt when you get to Pabst's. Far from it! Ask those Harlemites—those hardy men, with the solemn faces of folk who live forever in cold, northern places—and they will point their fingers toward the pack-ice of the Harlem River, and tell you there are cabarets "away up there." It is the Bronx they mean—that dark and fearsome region 'neath the Northern lights, whence so few travellers have returned. At the mention of the Bronx your taxi-driver's eye rolls horribly. So does his taximeter. Mutiny is in the air. Some one mentions a cabaret at Two Hundred and Thirteenth Street. Shivering, you picture what the place must be: a chill igloo, where caborigines eat blubber and dance the "polar-bear" and "penguin," throughout a night which lasts six months!

THE CABARET IN DARKEST HARLEM